Life Recalibrated

Life Recalibrated

Escape Auto-Pilot Living & Find Peace & Purpose in the Present

Dan Ferguson

Published by Game Changer Publishing

Paperback ISBN: 978-1-965653-87-6
Hardcover ISBN: 978-1-965653-51-7
Digital ISBN: 978-1-965653-52-4

www.GameChangerPublishing.com

DEDICATION

To my wife Amanda and my children Owen,
Kamryn, Anniston, and Lucy.
I wouldn't be here if it wasn't for you.

Read This First

Just to say thanks for buying and reading my book, I've put together a welcome video along with some helpful documents to support you on your journey with the book!

Scan the QR Code Here:

Life Recalibrated

*Escape Auto-Pilot Living & Find Peace
& Purpose in the Present*

Dan Ferguson

www.GameChangerPublishing.com

Acknowledgments

"I have always believed that YOU can have it all when YOU show up in life with FOCUS & INTENTIONALITY. This is contrary to what WE typically hear, which is to work hard and take time off. Dan Ferguson has written this book to show that YOU can work hard and achieve personal success. Buy the book, Implement the strategies, and live a more fulfilled life."

-Ben Newman
USA Today TOP 5 Mindset & Performance Coach
2x Wall Street Journal Bestseller

"Dan Ferguson has written the playbook on finding joy and fulfillment in everyday life! He is living his message to the fullest and is truly one of the most inspirational and engaged leaders I've had the privilege of knowing. If you want to find peace and purpose in the present, this book is for you!"

-Jordan Montgomery
USA Today Best-Selling Author
Top Keynote speaker
Performance coach

"Dan has written a gold mine of a book for anyone seeking a better work-life balance. He not only talks about it in this book, but he lives his life by it. I've known him for many years, and I have found him to be in a better place in his career and his family. If you want to be inspired to be better, please read this."

-Tommie Frazier
2X National Champion
Fiesta Bowl MVP 1996
2X Orange Bowl MVP (1994,1995)
Consensus All-American and Quarterback of the Year 1995

Table of Contents

INTRODUCTION

Is there a future where we can focus on being good at what we do within our careers or passions and be RICH at HOME instead of being rich at what we do and BROKE at HOME? I'm a conflicted workaholic who's still in recovery and fighting old workaholic habits. I haven't cracked it yet, but I'm in the process. My hope is to help others shorten their journey to figuring it out—or even prevent them from facing this issue—and to let them know they're not alone.

I'm also a father of four amazing children, a husband to a beautiful wife, and a son to not just two but three great, loving parents: my mother and father, and a stepfather, too. I'm a friend to many and a mentor to those I work with; whether they are my clients or new financial advisors I mentor within my business. I believe most would say I genuinely give a shit about other people. I'm also just an average Joe who has made a tremendous number of mistakes and will continue to make them—because I'm human.

Fortunately, I was lucky enough to find a career that gave me everything I ever wanted in life: challenges, constant learning, and the motivation and drive to succeed. I am a certified financial planner with a passion for helping others. My career allows people to truly learn about themselves and dig deep into their personal goals. Early on, I jumped into leadership within my organization because I knew I wanted to develop people and help them build the best life possible. However, along the way, I realized I was mostly focused on helping them build their professional lives. I wasn't paying enough attention to the personal side, and because of that, I made some mistakes. Those mistakes led me to the realization that, with focus and intentionality, you can have both: a well-rounded life that includes faith, health, work, personal fulfillment, and financial stability.

I wrote this book because I struggled to find techniques and strategies to reverse the course my life was on. I was headed for massive career success, but I felt empty inside. My career had become my identity, consuming me. I wanted to write this book for the same reason I got into developing new professionals: to shorten the duration of someone else's journey or to prevent them from making the same mistakes. If I could help even one person by writing this book, then all the time and money invested in it would be worth it.

Before this, I was a conflicted shell of myself, 24/7, never feeling fully present in any environment. I constantly felt like I should be somewhere else. I wanted to give people the tools and techniques to avoid this feeling. In the book, I've included stories and moments from different people, gathering them all in one place so that readers can hopefully advance far quicker than I did.

So, who is this book for? It's for anyone who's sick and tired of being sick and tired. It's for people who want to break the cycle, reprioritize their lives, and not have to give up what they've already built. It's also for those who want to become more present in their current moment, rather than always feeling conflicted. Social media, for instance, often creates feelings of imposter syndrome and insecurity. Every time I look at Instagram, it feels like everyone around me is on vacation, and it makes me feel like I'm never good enough or succeeding at anything. I want people to reach a place where they feel good about who they are and focus on measuring themselves against their own progress, aligning their priorities accordingly.

Everything I've implemented, I've learned from other great mentors and leaders. If anyone were to implement these ideas or recommendations, I'm confident they'd see a positive change in their life and happiness immediately.

There's a lot of content in this book, but I believe readers will gravitate toward a few areas that resonate deeply, where they'll say, "This is something I can do, and it would make a big impact." That's why I believe people should listen to me—not because I'm an expert or have it all figured out, but because I have techniques and strategies that can make an immediate difference in their lives.

What will readers get from this book? Hopefully, a better mindset and a strategy to help them move forward in life. But most importantly, they'll gain a clear vision of who they want to become, with actual steps to get there. Most of us have an idea of where we want to be, but we don't spend enough time thinking about who we truly want to become or how we would want our families to speak of us if we were no longer around. Once they figure that out, everything else becomes a process. My hope for the reader is that this book will change their life and the lives of those around them—whether it's a stranger, their children, their parents, or their significant other. The most important relationship they have is the one with themselves. And if you can begin to feel good about what you do and the inputs you put into your life, everything else improves as a byproduct.

But many of us are disappointed with who we are and don't know how to reverse that course. My hope is that readers will find a way to reverse that course, start feeling accomplished about what truly matters, and reprioritize their lives.

CHAPTER 1

BREAKING POINT

It was October 21st, 2014. I was sitting at a table with three colleagues from my study group, feeling incredibly blessed to have these individuals in my life. These were some of the best leaders I could learn from. First, there was Lee Patterson, who built a powerhouse agency in Phoenix and inspired everyone with his intense faith and belief in the Lord. He led with his heart. Then we had Ross Alisiani from Denver, our group organizer and a wildly talented leader who led his office with care, inclusiveness, and strategy. Lastly, there was Luke Madsen from Seattle, one of the most brilliant business minds I knew—and someone I considered my double in terms of personality. Luke led with forward-thinking strategies and an ability to develop deep relationships. We all worked for the same organization as directors and were at similar life stages at that time.

The purpose of our meeting was to collaborate on our businesses as well as our personal lives and the challenges we were facing. After we presented, we would give each other feedback and provide strategies for improvement. We were in Schaumburg,

Illinois, for a leadership conference, but our group chose to meet a day early to dive deep and learn from each other. These individuals were like family to me, and I trusted and respected them deeply. However, as they began giving their reports, I felt a knot tightening in the pit in my stomach, one that had been growing for some time. I was uneasy about who I was and where I was headed, both in my career and in my personal life. I felt like I was doing it all wrong despite the praise I was receiving for my professional results. I was determined to build a legacy in my business, believing that if I succeeded, my family would understand I did it all for them.

The week before this trip, I had traveled to Chicago to watch my beloved Nebraska Cornhuskers play Northwestern University (we won, by the way). That trip was with friends and my father, part of an annual Husker road trip we tried to take. Both trips felt necessary because I didn't want to let anyone down by not going. But the reality was that I had been away from my kids for five out of the last six days. I was feeling deeply conflicted about my priorities.

As Ross was presenting, I grew increasingly uncomfortable, dreading my turn. When it finally came, I started talking about my business from a professional standpoint. On paper, things were going well. By this point in my career, I had hit some significant benchmarks and risen to the top of my position within a Fortune 100 company. Normally, when it was my turn to present, people would lean in, eager to hear what we were doing in Nebraska to achieve such great results. But partway through my presentation, I just stopped and stared at my screen. The weight I had been carrying finally broke me. I felt mentally paralyzed and couldn't move. A wave of emotions crashed over me, and I'm not embarrassed to admit it—I started bawling. I told them the realization that had been gnawing at me for so long: I was officially broke at home.

I wasn't living a life that felt right to me, and I had to take responsibility for that. It was the result of my own choices. I realized that my focus had been misdirected. I was known as the guy who wanted to have fun while balancing my social life, being a parent, and being a highly productive leader. But regret and resentment had been building with every decision I made. I was trying to fit the sand, rocks, pebbles, and water into the jar in the wrong order, and it simply wouldn't work. My priorities were completely out of alignment.

I had become a shell of myself, constantly conflicted and never feeling like I was where I should be. Even though I was surrounded by people, I felt completely alone. I realized that I was an insecure people pleaser, trying to make everyone think things were going great when, in reality, I was broken inside. And yet, people wanted to learn from *me*?

In defense of my colleagues, besides my study group, not many people were asking how I was doing at home. They were more interested in hearing about my strategies for developing new advisors and growing the business. I thought the success I was having required me to balance everything—building my personal business, serving my clients, and leading our office. I had to show everyone the way, be the first one in the office, work hard all day, and leave only when the work was done. The problem was the work never stopped. I had no boundaries, no way to end the cycle. If there was an opportunity to grow my business, I would make the sacrifice. I attended happy hours, went to conferences, took late-night appointments, and even built a consulting practice on the side, where other offices paid me to teach them what we were doing to achieve results. The success was going to my head, creating an ego and an image I felt I had to uphold. I thought I was providing for my family in the best way possible by pouring myself into my work, believing it would give us the life we wanted.

But I was wrong. It went against my values, yet I didn't know how to stop. Not everyone around me was making the same sacrifices, but I had blinders on and couldn't see it. At one point, I gave a presentation at a symposium about our internship program. The organizers, who had flown me in, surprised me with a gift: a shirt that said *"Ferguson World Tour"* on it, with dates and locations on the back listing all the places I had spoken. When I saw it, I felt empty inside. Instead of feeling successful, I felt like they were showing me all the dates and times I had been away from the most important people in my life. It was a harsh reality check.

Wining and Dining Was Part of the Role

Whenever I was at a work conference, out with clients, out with friends, or speaking, I was having cocktails to socialize. It felt like part of the role, right? But I was wrong. It was a cycle that I had control over, yet I didn't want anyone to know I was struggling—or worse, that I didn't want to "have fun" with them. At the end of the night, when I lay down, I felt a rush of emotions that left me tossing and turning, conflicted, and unable to sleep. Every morning, I woke up feeling like an imposter. Why would anyone want to listen to what I had to say? As these feelings faded throughout the day, I told myself it was just because of the drinks from the night before—a story I repeated over and over again. I thought it was normal; I thought everyone experienced these emotions.

What Should Have Been Rock Bottom

In February 2011, I was out socializing with co-workers and colleagues in Lincoln, Nebraska. I was 29 at the time, and my ego was at its peak—I was "living it up." On my way home, I was pulled over and charged with a DUI. Shouldn't that have been the moment when I knew I had to change? Unfortunately, I still believed this would blow over—that it wasn't a big deal. That's how big my ego was. When I woke up, I had to face the reality of the DUI, and I was ashamed of myself. I was placed under strict professional boundaries, and it was a warning. Luckily, I was able to keep my job, but they were watching me. Sure, I made some short-term changes, but I still didn't feel like I'd hit rock bottom. I was still successful in my business, and over time, as the shame faded and people forgot, I went back to my old ways. I just became more cautious, avoiding driving after drinking, but I hadn't truly hit rock bottom.

Values Reality Check

Not long after, I attended a conference centered around

coaching new advisors. The presenter asked us to identify our top four values. He gave us a list of over 40 potential values to choose from, and I wrote down that my number one value was family. I felt good about that. After we completed the exercise, he asked two powerful questions: "*How many of you listed 'family' as your top value?*" Many of us raised our hands. Then he asked, "*Does your checkbook reflect it?*" That hit me like a ton of bricks. His point was that most people say family is their top value, but few actually live by it. If you looked at my checkbook, it would have reflected all the wrong priorities. At that moment, I felt like a fraud, struggling with a deep moral conflict.

I had made a lot of bad decisions—decisions that had led to a divorce, a DUI, and constant feelings of conflict about who I was and where I was headed. Did that mean I had wasted all my time focusing on my business or social life? No. Did it mean I didn't love my children? Absolutely not. I was just out of alignment. I needed to recalibrate and become clear about where I was going. The best asset I had was time, and I'm thankful for everything I went through, but I knew it was time to reverse course. I knew it wouldn't be easy, as I was stuck in a routine I didn't know how to break. The people I surrounded myself with—both in and outside of my profession— were living similarly, pouring themselves into their businesses, doing whatever it took to succeed. I didn't want to walk away from these individuals out of a sense of loyalty, but I realized that if I could make the necessary changes, maybe I could help them, too.

I realized that even when I was home, I was never truly *present*.
I was always thinking about work. Now, here I was in Schaumburg,
Illinois, learning from some of the best minds in our business, and
all I could think about was home. I didn't know where to go or where
to start. Should I talk to a counselor? Hire a life coach? Find a book
to help me figure this out? As I started asking questions and looking
for answers, I realized I wasn't alone. I knew it was time to break the
cycle, but I also couldn't ignore the collateral beauty that had come
from my decisions.

I had built a strong business that I could maintain. I had proven
results that could inspire confidence in those who worked with me
in the future. In 2013, I took a break from life and went on a trip to
Kansas City with friends. While waiting for a table at a restaurant, I
met the love of my life, Amanda, who is now my wife. I can't look
back and say that nothing good came from my past decisions, but I
do know that without hitting that breaking point, I might never have
fixed things.

Over the next eight chapters, I'm going to share ideas and
strategies about how I got my life back on track and the impact it has
had on me and those around me. I'll include action items at the end
of some chapters to provide a framework for making change. One
of the best exercises when you know some systems are broken is a
"Start, Stop, Continue" exercise. The name is self-explanatory: it's
about identifying what you need to start doing, what you need to
stop doing, and what you need to continue doing. Empty your mind,
and take time to think about each area of your life. What do you

really need to start doing? What eats at you when you do it and needs to stop? What's working well that you need to continue?

Start

_____

_____

_____

_____

_____

Stop

_____

_____

_____

_____

_____

Continue

_____

_____

_____

_____

_____

_____

CHAPTER 2

ACCOUNTABILITY PARTNERS

Recently, the CEO of our company, John Schlifske, was on Ben Beshear's *Life, Money, and Living Well* Podcast, and he said something that summed up how I felt in 2014, along with how I wanted to craft my life. He said, "Our company helps clients begin to save money by following a simple strategy called paying yourself first. Some clients will spend their money and try to save what's left over, while others will save the first 10%–20% and then spend what's left over. What I did was the same thing for my family. I wanted them to get the best of me, and everyone else got the bottom compared to me pouring into everything else, leaving my family with what was left over." I felt the same way—my family was getting what was left over. I needed to start building the life I wanted, but I didn't know how. In the following, I'll begin to lay out the process we went through and explore the collateral beauty of the people who entered my life at just the right times.

Clarity Around the WHAT

After completing the Start, Stop, Continue exercise, I really identified what I needed to start doing. One of the main things I needed to do was find strong accountability partners—people who would challenge me. I knew I needed to find a coach, whether a life coach or a professional coach. I had always been hesitant to hire a coach because of the financial commitment, but I also knew I was a very uncoachable individual. I was introduced to a business coach named Tricia Hamilton from the East Coast. Tricia had a knack for working with "uncoachable shitheads." When I met with Tricia, I carried a lot of mistrust and frustration, which I shared with her.

> **Me:** *Why should I trust you? I was introduced to you by someone I am lacking trust with.*

> **Tricia:** *You don't have to trust me, and quite frankly, I don't want you to yet. However, if you give me enough time, I'll earn your trust. But I will also challenge you harder than anyone ever has.*

Her answer was perfect for me. She identified very quickly that I have always bluffed everyone and never really let anyone in, and she wanted to learn why. Tricia became an extremely key figure for me from that moment on. She was very patient with me, and she coached me hard, but she walked me through a two-piece exercise that truly helped me connect the right side of my brain with the left side. The left side of our brain controls our logic; it tells us all what we "should do." The right side of our brain controls our emotions, which is what we "want to do." Emotion is seven times more powerful than logic; if they are conflicting with each other, our right side normally wins. The power of change will happen when both sides of the brain work together rather than conflicting with each other. Tricia wanted to help capture my current and future emotions and use them as fuel. She explained to me that it's almost like the first step of Alcoholics Anonymous: it's admitting that you're powerless over the drug.

> *Tricia: For the first step, I want you to capture all the current emotions you have about your life. I want you to explain all the items you put on your list for the items you want to stop doing. I want you to be as clear as you can and finally come clean with what you are not proud of, and I want you to title this "The Moment."*

I wrote down everything; I didn't sugarcoat it. I beat the crap out of myself and put all my faults and mistakes on the table. I was very honest with where I was at in life. Every time I read it, it made a lump in my throat, and I couldn't believe that it had reached that point.

> *Tricia: Now that you have completed this, I want you to tell me where you are going. I want you to really identify and lay out very clearly who you want to be.*

Tricia wanted me to really dig into my Start, Stop, Continue exercise, and a few things became very clear about what needed to change. It felt like the most liberating process as I laid out my rock-bottom feelings and became so connected with my future. It was like I finally left all the baggage, stress, and mistakes at the door and was able to move on. Tricia kept digging and asking me more about why I had listed all these things and what it would mean if they came true. She walked me through questions like, "*What do you want your kids to say about you? If you passed away tomorrow and people were talking about you, what do you want them to say?*"

One of the best ways to craft a vision is to start writing down things you REALLY WANT and then put the word "AND" after each one, continuing until you run out of "ANDS." After that, I rated each on a scale of 1–5, with 5 being the most important and 1 being feel-good items that didn't carry much weight. I finally compiled the top items and created a story about the future and all the changes I had made, focusing on how I would feel. I wanted to connect to that future moment and feel the emotions—like goosebumps—of what it would be like once it happened. Throughout this book, I'll refer to this as "clarity" because the first step to any major change in behavior is becoming clear on where you're going. One of my favorite quotes is from Helen Keller: "There is only one thing worse than being blind. It's being able to see and having no vision." I truly feel that if you believe strongly in who you are going to become, you can begin to forget who you are today.

The What, the How, and the Why

After I became clear on WHAT I wanted, I needed to connect with WHY I wanted it, and then figure out HOW to achieve it. The WHY is the emotional pull. During this process, I learned a lot about myself, and I also learned from key people in my life. I'm going to reference many of those key moments and the impact they had. I knew I needed to be patient and have a plan, or I would slip back into old habits and conflicting thoughts. Does that mean I had to drop my friends, quit my job, change my phone number, and run away from life? No, it didn't. However, I knew that old habits die hard, and it was going to take a lot of work to break them.

There was a movie I watched at just the right time. It brought out almost every emotion—laughter, sadness, even some tears. The movie was *Click* with Adam Sandler.[1] Even though it was a comedy, it rocked me to my core. I watched it through a different lens than most. The movie gave me insight into what I might become as I got older: RICH in my career but BROKE at home. I wanted to be GOOD at my job but RICH at home. In the movie, the character is focused on hitting a certain career milestone, but his personal life gets in the way. He's given a remote control that lets him fast-forward through life, skipping over being sick, fighting with his wife, family dinners, building a treehouse for his kids, etc.

Eventually, the remote starts fast-forwarding automatically, stopping only for his promotions. He's physically present with his family but mentally disconnected. By the end, his kids are grown, he's divorced, the stepdad becomes the male figure in their lives, and his son repeats the same pattern—focused only on work. He's alone but successful in his career. That's what's important, right? (Sorry if I've spoiled the movie if you were planning to rent it!) He ends up waking up and realizing it was all a dream, coming home with new

---

[1] Coraci, Frank, director. *Click*. Sony Pictures, 2006.

energy to embrace the life he's in. That's the emotion I was experiencing in 2014. Everything became clear, and I realized I had the time to change my trajectory.

Leaning Into My Faith

One of the most impactful conversations I've ever had was with a good friend of mine who is a pastor at our church, Pastor Josh. Josh is someone I've always looked up to and respected deeply. I sat down with him and shared where I was mentally and emotionally. I told him about my breakdown at the leadership conference, my divorce, and my fear of splitting time with my kids and them resenting me. I was afraid of living with regret. He asked me standard questions about work and life, almost as though he was fact-finding to see how real I was being about the issue. Then Josh said something that has been burned into my brain ever since. He started sharing a story:

> **Josh:** *I sit down with quite a few people each year who need a little faith in their life, and most of the people I meet with are on hospice and don't have long to live. When I sit down with these individuals, no matter what age they are, I always ask them to tell me about their life. To this day, I've never had one person tell me about the year they hit their sales goal or the year they finally made $500,000 or more. The only thing they talk about are the experiences they had with their family—or the experiences they missed with their family, and how much regret they have about it.*

It was like a bullet hitting me in the chest.

Me: Josh, that's where I'm at. I'm operating like an iPhone.

Josh: What does that mean?

Me: Well, if I'm an iPhone and I have all my apps up and running, but then I put my phone down, what's it doing?

Josh: It's burning its battery.

Me: Exactly. Am I using these applications or my phone at that time?

Josh: No.

Me: Josh, I'm burning my battery. I'm always thinking of something else, no matter what situation I'm in. And I'm watching my life slip by because I'm always building toward something in the future. Quite frankly, I don't even know what that something is. But I do know that what I'm doing at work is working, and I'm getting some success. At the same time, I know I'm not doing what I need to be doing at home, so I feel like I'm going to work to avoid the hard work at home.

Josh: Well, how are you going to fix that?

Me: That's what I'm working on right now.

Josh: As you begin your journey to restore the things you want to work on, just remember this: the best relationships I've ever seen are the ones where they always have something to look forward to.

Me: *What do you mean?*

Josh: *When you're on a trip with your family or doing something together, don't ever act like it's the last time you're going to do it. Talk about where you're going to go next.*

I don't think I fully grasped the importance of that last comment in the moment. It becomes a very crucial part of a future chapter. Josh really wanted me to build healthy relationships with my family and not just focus on a quick fix. He wanted me to focus on being a change agent, finding ways to build memories and live the life we want.

Accountability Around My WHY

At this time, I was engaged to my best friend and one of my most important accountability partners, Amanda. Through her own life experience, she did not want to be married to a man who prioritized his career more than his family. She was more than willing to sacrifice potential future income to make sure we were living according to our values. I was so blessed to find someone who wanted my actions and values to align. Without her support, this may have been an impossible task.

I was having such a tough time coming to terms with not being able to see my kids every day. I was trying to balance a relatively new relationship, providing for my kids, and implementing all the changes I needed to make. Amanda's advice immediately changed the way I viewed my relationship with the kids.

> **Me:** *I hate not being able to see my kids every day, and it's really impacting me. It makes me feel like I failed them.*

> **Amanda:** *You may never be able to make up the days you missed, but you can make up the minutes.*

She made such an incredible point. I had to accept the position I was in, but at the same time, I needed to maximize it. If I spent my time focusing on the part that was out of my control, which was the actual days the kids were with their mother, it would weigh me down. Instead, I needed to make every minute I had with them count. I made a commitment then and there that every chance I had with my kids would be spent focusing solely on them. I made sure that I never gave up my time with the kids unless it was a mandatory commitment. I stayed present and focused on them when they were with us. I didn't want to look back and regret my decisions because my children are my priority. Amanda was the most critical piece in helping me not revert to who I had been. I was excited to finish work every day and go home to my family, not only physically but mentally as well.

Developing Strategies

Identifying the problem and envisioning the future is 10% of the battle. Executing the plan is the other 90%. So I was willing to go public and share this with people. I was clear about the mistakes I had made and who I wanted to become. I had a clear vision, but I knew it wouldn't be fixed in a day. I knew I would have to fully commit to this process. It took embracing a significant amount of humility and facing judgment because here I was: a man in the business of giving advice, yet I was divorced, had gotten a DUI, and my priorities were misaligned.

Going public and owning my mistakes was liberating, to say the least. I no longer had to pretend that everything was okay or that there wasn't a problem. However, that didn't stop the naysayers from coming out of the woodwork to try and pull me back to who I was. That's when I started to notice that misery loves company.

The individuals who were also broken at home tried to bring me down. I found myself arguing and defending myself against peer pressure. But I realized that you should never argue with an idiot— they'll drag you down to their level and beat you with experience. So, I just let it roll off my chest because I was finally clear about who I wanted to become.

There are two ways to build the biggest building in town: either build the biggest building or tear down every other building that's bigger than yours. I was ready to build my best life. You may have to face hard realities about the people around you. And if someone is going to pull you down rather than lift you up, you'll have to either change the people you're with—or change the people you're with.

Action Items

(Scan the QR Code for Documents and for Authors Thoughts on Completing)

1. Complete the "Moment Exercise."

2. Pick the time frame in the future (whether it be one, three, or five years) and spend time writing a very clear vision.

3. Share both of these with someone you trust and respect.

CHAPTER 3

PRIORITY MANAGEMENT

I had a vision that needed a strategy to be sustainable because just wanting change wouldn't work. I needed to start somewhere and make this my new reality. I'm going to lay out the tactical steps we began to implement that helped shape this into reality. One of the most critical changes I made was finally becoming clear on what my top priorities were. I started to realize there was a significant difference between time management and priority management. Time management involves managing all my duties as a dad, husband, friend, and professional, which can make everything seem equally important. When I focused too much on what fed the professional "machine," my priorities quickly fell out of alignment. I felt like I was constantly shifting things around to make everyone happy.

Priority management, on the other hand, meant holding firm to my top priorities that aligned with the vision of the person I wanted to be. Growing my business and being home for family dinners did not carry the same weight. While my business was important, it wasn't as important as the time commitments I made to my family.

Before October 21st, 2014, my values were out of alignment, and I had a hard time keeping them straight. I was weak in managing my days effectively, often going home feeling like an iPhone burning its battery. I knew the power was in the calendar. I needed to build a calendar that I would be proud of, one that maximized my time and provided consistency. I also needed to learn to say no to the right things.

Parental Advice

My mom and dad were full of great advice as I was growing up. My mom always reminded us about the Golden Rule, and I try to embody this in everything I do. She would also frequently say, "Two wrongs don't make a right. People are going to hurt you, and they will let you down. Getting even isn't the answer."

My dad gave me a piece of advice early in my career that became even more important when priority management became my focus. It was in 2005. I was one year into the business, still a new advisor trying to make it. It was a Wednesday afternoon, and my friends called to say they had secured a tee time at Firethorn, one of the nicest courses in Lincoln. They asked if I wanted to join them, and the obvious answer was "YES!" How could I not go? My calendar was pretty open, so I figured I'd head out to play. As I was driving there, I called my dad because I thought he'd be excited to hear I was going to play such a great course. My dad loves golf, and it was a way we connected.

Me: *I'm actually on my way out to Firethorn to golf with Jim and Mitch.*

Dad: *Huh, that's weird.*

Me: *What do you mean, that's weird?*

Dad: *I thought the career you're in was very difficult, and it's hard to make it.*

Me: *Yeah, it is, but I don't have any appointments for the rest of the day. One of the benefits of my career is that I have some independence and flexibility.*

Dad: *Hmm. You know you've grown up when you have the ability to say no. If you're in one of the toughest businesses to make it in and you have half a day left, you should really ask yourself, "Should I really be doing this right now?"*

I felt dumb, but I knew he was right. I needed that tough message. So, I said, "You're probably right." At that moment, I pulled over, texted my friends, and told them I wasn't going to make it. They didn't push back—they understood. I went back to work, got some things done, and grew my business. That lesson stuck with me, but I know I wasn't always consistent in applying it. When it came to priority management, the word "no" became key. It's a muscle I needed to work on and stick to.

Time Blocking

I needed to build a calendar that reflected my priorities. When I sat down with my schedule, the first thing I did was take a blank calendar and build out my ideal lifestyle, aligned with my vision. The first step was to block out my firm personal commitments. I set aside from 3:00 p.m. to 10:00 p.m. on the days I had my kids and labeled it "KIDS." I've kept this in place for years now. Initially, it was surprisingly hard to hold those commitments. I frequently got questions like, "Hey, your calendar says you have your kids on Thursday, but is there any way you can help me with a case at 6:00?" People weren't trying to be rude or disrespectful, it was just habit. Normally, I would have been a people pleaser and found a way to make it work.

If your priorities stay in alignment, you'll begin to see your energy and capacity increase to new levels. An ideal calendar works well, but you can't expect it to be perfect—things come up. Still, I do everything I can to hold it firm. I was once told that an ideal calendar that holds true 80% of the time is a massive success. I began making modifications along the way, like scheduling date nights one to three times a month and other personal commitments. The second step was building in mandatory professional meetings. The third step was setting the professional inputs necessary to run a strong business.

If you want an effective strategy for day-to-day productivity, don't label time blocks too generically. For example, in our business, we block time for reaching out to clients. I saw many advisors label it "*phoning time*," which didn't necessarily correlate with measurable intentionality. I labeled that same time block "Book five appointments" because it eliminated mediocre work. Finally, I broke everything down into 1-hour and 15-minute meeting slots for running my practice. This helped me see how much time I had left to grow my client base.

Oddly, after building my priorities and seeing the time left over, I was shocked. I realized I had more than enough time to perform at a high level without sacrificing what was truly important. Earlier, I referenced putting the rocks, pebbles, sand, and water in the jar in the wrong order. My time with my family was my *rocks*, the *pebbles* were mandatory business meetings, the *sand* was my controllable inputs for my business I listed daily, and the *water* was running my business, seeing clients. When I led with my rocks first, everything fit correctly this time. I color-coded my schedule, with the darkest colors representing higher priorities. It served as a constant reminder that whenever I moved a lighter-colored appointment into a slot that had a darker color, I needed to re-evaluate why I felt that was necessary. Putting some level of visual accountability always made me think twice. It's a small detail with a big impact.

The Power of Holding Others Accountable

I had an advisor I was working with who wanted to build a better connection with his grandfather. He told me that his grandpa was his number one fan during his high school days, but ever since he moved away, they had lost contact. We started every coaching session with one question: "Have you talked to your grandpa this week?" If the answer was no, I would stop our session and tell him to make the call, and we'd pick back up after it was done. As he became more connected to his grandfather, he became more motivated in his business. I saw this as a huge missing piece in his development. I built stronger connections with each person I developed because I took the time to get to know them. I wanted to figure out what they really wanted, but most importantly, I didn't want them to think my only focus was their professional life. I wanted them to become the person they wanted to be outside of work. Operating outside of your priorities will lead to a lack of productivity, loss of energy, and a decline in mental health. If my main duty as a mentor was to hold them accountable to their top priorities, sign me up!

What's the Harm in a Happy Hour?

What's the harm in the occasional happy hour? For me, there was a lot of harm. I built a schedule to stick to my top priorities, but my priorities were constantly challenged. As I mentioned earlier, I'm a people pleaser. I would receive an invite to a social event, and it was always hard to say no. I didn't want that person to feel like they weren't important to me. If I could make them happy and feel important while also growing my business, it seemed like the right decision. For so long, I played that game, but then I realized it was taking away from a bigger priority.

I delivered a podcast on this topic, and I'll go a little deeper into it. A gentleman named John asked me to hop on my first podcast about three years ago.

Dan Ferguson joins John Mortgage Major on the Aksarben Mortgage Podcast.

Scan the QR Code to Access:

Me: John, why did you ask me to come on your podcast?

John: I just want to learn from you because you're one of the weirdest professionals I know.

Me: Ha, I don't know if that's a good thing, but what do you mean?

John: You literally say no to every event I invite you to. I'm just curious because it seems like your business is going well, but you attend very few events that could help grow your business.

Me: Well, John, everything you invite me to is either on a Wednesday or Thursday.

John: Okay, and?

Me: John, I don't work after 3 p.m. on Wednesdays or Thursdays.

John: Why?

Me: Those are the days I pick my kids up from school.

Now John understood that picking my kids up from school was important. What he didn't understand was why I had to be the one. Couldn't my wife pick them up?

Me: If I say yes to a networking event you set up, it means I'm saying no to my kids. If my kids ran out of school expecting me to be there and saw my wife instead, it would send the wrong message. Of course, Amanda would help, but that could have a drastic impact on my relationship with my kids long term. I don't want to set the example that I'm always going to choose growing my business over growing my relationship with them.

I could tell that had an impact on John because I've noticed a lot of changes in how he builds out his schedule. I told him that I have priorities that are extremely important to me, and I'm not going to skip out on them going forward.

Don't Overstay Your Welcome

My doctor has always told me that everything in life is better when done in moderation. He says that junk food, socializing, work, alone time—everything is fine if done in moderation. I still have hobbies outside of my career and family, and I want to enjoy my passions, but I also want to put boundaries around them. My father liked to golf when I was growing up, and he sometimes spent a lot of time on the golf course. That was his passion and his way of socializing, which was his choice. I still remember it like it was yesterday: my dad had plastic golf balls in an old coffee can, and he dumped them into the yard when I was little and said, "*When you can hit these straight, I'll take you golfing.*" I yearned for that connection with my dad as a child. In return, I spent so much time trying to hit those plastic balls straight. It was a difficult task, but I wouldn't quit until I finally did it. I became a pretty good golfer in high school and have maintained the skill since then.

I still want to enjoy golf, but I never want it to impact my relationships. I'll play during normal business hours if I play during the week. If I play on the weekend for leisure, I want to be home by lunch, or my family will ride along and enjoy it with me. When it becomes an option to go home, I go. This last part is key for me, and it also makes me a bit of a buzzkill. For example, if I play on a Friday with clients or friends, I'm focused on my company and the game. I don't spend time on my phone stressing about work or taking calls. But when the round is over and everyone wants to head in for a drink or food, that's when I head home. I sometimes catch flak for never hanging out, but I don't blame anyone else. This is a key thing that most men do—they blame their spouse, etc. For me, I just say, "Hey guys, I'm heading home, but by all means, stick around and enjoy." When they say, "Oh, come on in for one," it's a simple "No, I'm good. I'd rather head home, but thanks." And it's done.

However, if the kids are still in school and Amanda is working, then sure, I'll spend time with my company because they're a priority. But if I have a bigger priority at home expecting me, it's no question. If I hold my boundaries, it eliminates the possibility of my wife or kids becoming resentful of one of my passions.

Staying focused on priority management and creating boundaries to prevent one priority from cannibalizing another helped me clear out the mental clutter and recharge my battery.

Action Item: Time Blocking Steps

1. Build in your personal priorities (Rocks).

2. Build in mandatory work meetings (Pebbles).

3. Build in your daily intentions and label them correctly (Sand).

4. Use the rest of the time to complete the meetings that grow your business (Water).

Takeaways

- Identifying the difference between time management and priority management.

- You know you have grown up when you have the ability to say no.

- Have as much passion for holding others to their priorities as you do your own.

- Saying yes to one thing means you are saying no to another.

- Firm boundaries can eliminate resentment.

CHAPTER 4

YES MENTALITY

One of the worst things about draining my battery all day was that I would go home with a negative attitude. Most of the time, I let it affect me more than it should have. Another movie that had a far bigger impact on me than any other was *Yes Man*.[2] I was saying yes to the wrong things, which meant I was saying no to the wrong things. I needed to say yes to the right things. So let's paint a picture.

If you're currently raising children, I believe you will connect with this section. Let's assume I've had a long day at work. I just got home, changed into comfy clothes, and I'm ready to relax for the day. The couch or chair is so comfortable, my phone is charging, and dinner is on my mind. My six-year-old runs up to me and says, "Dad, can we…?" And let's just stop right there. For the longest time, my mindset would immediately go to, "*Not right now*," because I was tired. I had been burning my battery all day long and wasn't recharging it. I had just gotten home, and I wanted to relax. So many of us experience this.

---

[2] Reed, Peyton, director. *Yes Man*. Warner Bros, 2008.

So I was saying yes to all the stuff that happened throughout the day, but when my six-year-old wanted to spend time with me, my answer was, "*Not right now*"? Sadly, she would walk away with her head hanging low, possibly feeling like she had done something wrong. Every time, it made me feel like a horrible parent. Does that mean I currently say yes to everything? Of course not. I'm not going to give my kids a "Yes Day" to everything because they would never learn boundaries. The change I wanted to make was to think "yes" before I thought "no." I didn't know exactly how to work on this.

How Lucky I Am

I definitely don't want to paint a grim picture, but I had to really embrace gratitude and realize how lucky I was. If something bad happened to any of my kids and I never got that question again, I know I would think, "*What I wouldn't give to go outside and play basketball with Owen or Anniston, to go to the park with Lucy, or to practice stunting with Kamryn.*" Saying yes, or at least developing that mindset, filled my bucket. It did the reverse of what I expected—it gave me energy. I can't remember any scenario where I said yes and regretted it. However, I do regret shutting down their requests many times, and I had to find a way to stop that and celebrate how lucky I was.

I put a challenge out to anyone reading this: for the next 48 hours, whenever your kids ask you, "Can we...?" try to catch yourself from saying no immediately. Lean into it because when you say yes, weird things start to happen, and suddenly, it shows up more in your life.

As I started talking openly and creating dialogue with friends, co-workers, or family about the Yes Man mentality, it created an extremely powerful bond between us. It was like the unspoken conversation that most people weren't having with others. It seemed that almost everyone was also thinking "not right now" as their first thought, and it made them feel like a bad parent. We would discuss how we were just sick and tired of feeling sick and tired all the time. Once I started sharing with them the changes I was making, they would say, "*I need to try that. I just feel tired, but also like I'm a terrible parent.*" I would let them know that they were not a bad parent, but we just get stuck in patterns and attitudes that need to be recalibrated.

No Regrets

I had a formal leader who retired a few years ago named Mike Tews. Mike was a great leader and a driver of results, but he constantly reminded our leadership team that some of the best investments you can make are the time and experiences you have with your family. He told us that one of his biggest goals in life was to send his kids to college without having any regrets. If you sit down and complain about the difficulty of raising kids with someone who has adult children, it's almost guaranteed they'll say, with a certain level of pain, "*I miss those days—they go so fast.*" For me, this really put things in perspective. We always seem to want to be in a different place in life than the one we're currently in.

I embraced this and accepted that our life is chaotic, but I wouldn't want it any other way. It helped me adopt the mindset of "Why not?" We really only get a few years of being asked to dance with our young ones, to go to the park, to chase bubbles, or to drive them to their commitments. My son Owen is currently 22 years old. When he was in middle and high school, he was all teenage boy. One of the things that drove Amanda and me bonkers was that Owen would constantly yell while playing video games. We would yell downstairs for him to keep it down. Then, Owen went to college in 2020. It took about a month of him being gone for me to say, "*I'd love to hear him yelling in the basement at his Xbox again.*" We love having Owen around, and we missed everything about him when he was gone. That experience helped Amanda and me embrace the moment of having a house full of kids.

The kids are only going to ask us to hang out with them for so long before they're gone. So let's roll with the punches and get involved in their world.

Action Item

Put the book down right now and find the one person who asks the most of you. It can be a child, wife, parent, sibling, or even a roommate. Identify one thing they ask of you the most that you normally decline doing. Now go and do it.

Afterward, just write down how it made you feel. Was it as bad as you expected? Or did you use some energy to gain more back?

_____

_____

_____

_____

_____

_____

_____

CHAPTER 5

BEING INTENTIONAL

Now that I had developed the calendar to live by my priorities, everything was going to fall into place, right? Absolutely not. I was just as guilty as everyone else of merely showing up. In this chapter, I want to talk more about showing up with intentionality every chance you get. We're never going to be able to create more hours in a day, but we can make up for the minutes by taking advantage of the opportunities that are right in front of us. I wanted my family to get the best I had to give, not just my leftovers.

My advice is to focus on your career because it is the fuel that supports your experiences with your family. Your career should operate like food. Some people view food as pleasure, while others view it as fuel. Those who see food as fuel are careful about what they put into their bodies, and in return, they have more energy, better health, and seem happier in general. The same goes for your career: if you have boundaries and operate efficiently, you'll see similar benefits. On the contrary, if someone indulges in food purely for pleasure, it may feel good in the moment, but afterward, they're left with poor health, exhaustion, and mental fatigue, often leading to regret. If you pour too much into your career, it will destroy your health, relationships, and mental well-being.

I started looking at how I was spending my time with my family. I knew I needed to adjust how I was showing up and ensure they were getting the best of me. Once I identified what I wanted to fix, I needed to put a plan into action. Just being clear in my vision was 10% of the work; the other 90% is executing on priorities. How could I think differently about my current environment? How could I show up better for the ones I love the most?

Invest Time in Parenting

I attended a presentation by a great leader named Keith, and as he neared the end, the questions started. His presentation was impactful because it didn't just focus on professional ideas—he emphasized the personal side, which was refreshing.

Me: Keith, what is the best book you have ever read?

Keith: Can you provide more context? Are you asking about the best book to help grow my business or the one that had the biggest impact on my life?

Me: Well, the one that had the biggest impact on your life?

Keith: Hands down, Strong Fathers, Strong Daughters by Meg Meeker.[3]

---

[3] Meeker, Margaret J. *Strong Fathers, Strong Daughters: 10 Secrets Every Father Should Know.* Regnery Publishing, a Division of Salem Media Group, 2017.

Meg Meeker is a childhood psychologist who compiled a lot of information about the impact of a dad being present in his daughter's life. She explains how a girl's relationship with her father is the most impactful one she'll ever have. Having a present father (or not) can completely change the trajectory of their life and how they view relationships. At this time, Kamryn and Anniston were still very young, so I realized I needed to invest the time to read this book. *Strong Fathers, Strong Daughters* confirmed my belief that I needed to be present and intentional with my relationship with them.

Like most parents, I feel like the majority of the time I spend with my children is in the car: driving them to and from camps, practice, school, and other extracurricular activities. When I started looking at how much time we spent on these trips, I realized how much opportunity I had been overlooking. I began to take advantage of those moments because most of us rush through life too fast. We look forward to the day when our kids are self-sufficient and can drive themselves to and from sports, but when that day comes, we often wish we could have those moments back.

How did I lean into my time with the kids? One of the first and most important changes we made was turning off the radio. I wanted to become an expert at asking questions and creating a healthy dialogue. I didn't want our communication to be superficial because I wasn't asking the right questions. I focused on asking open-ended questions that made them think and respond with more than one word. When I was going through the motions, it was more like,

"*How was school?*" and the response would be "*Good.*" To help change that, Amanda and I bought a box of conversation cards for kids to spice up our talks. These fun questions got them talking and gave me the chance to learn more about them and their wild ideas. At first, I thought our teenager would roll her eyes at the idea, but during a family dinner, our 15-year-old said, "*We should get out the question cards.*" It was music to my ears.

On our drive to the Ferguson family vacation this year, I had a 13-year-old and two 15-year-old girls in my car. I pulled out the conversation cards to change up the energy, and we talked for two hours straight with the radio off. It's a tremendous technique I wish I had used earlier. Any kind of cards that prompt conversation can be perfect. If you really want to know how your first-grader is doing, ask them who they sat with at lunch and why, who they played with at recess and why, or who they'd invite for a sleepover and why. I also asked if they noticed anyone being unfriendly to others and why. Our children, unfortunately, don't communicate like we did growing up.

Of course, some drives were just for singing our heads off to our favorite songs. If you start any song from *The Greatest Showman* soundtrack, I've got it covered. I believe everyone goes through a Greatest Showman phase at some point. If my kids wanted me to sing a duet with them, I was all in. It wasn't all about their music, though. I was able to introduce them to my music—rock and roll. I gave them the history of music and explained why I liked certain bands. I wanted them to learn about me, my childhood, and the struggles I went through. Once I started sharing the history of my emotions and how grunge music helped me in the '90s, or how the Foo Fighters were formed and my experiences seeing them live, our conversations deepened, bringing us closer. I wanted my kids to feel like they had a safe space to share their lives with me.

That doesn't mean I was perfect at communication. At first, I would go into dad mode and offer solutions to all their problems. That's the fastest way to shut down my daughters and their willingness to open up. Learning how to communicate with them was difficult at first, but I wanted a deeper connection with them because it may influence the man they choose to marry. If they shared a problem they were facing, I would ask, *"How do you want me to show up right now?"* If they said they just wanted me to listen, I would listen and let them air out whatever they wanted to get off their chest. I wanted them to have a safe space to have somebody to communicate with on our way to school because not only did I want them to know that I cared, but I wanted them to learn how to express their feelings. So I would get in the vehicle, we would be heading 20 minutes to our practice or whatever it was, and I would say, *"Tell me what's going on in your world right now that's causing you stress or anxiety."* And I would also reference that I was showing up to listen, not to solve problems, and that nothing was off limits. At first, it took them a while to open up, but it became a very good safe haven in which they could share the things that they were struggling with. Shockingly, every once in a while, they would even ask for my opinion or advice. That took our relationship from zero to 60 extremely quickly.

Before making this change, I would get into the car and let the kids know I had a few calls to return, asking them to keep it down. That communication made them feel unimportant, which is the absolute last feeling I ever want my kids to have.

Quality Time

Strong Fathers, Strong Daughters also emphasizes the importance of one-on-one time with parents. One of the best things we did was that Amanda and I began having kids' date nights. I would ask the kids to pick something they wanted to do, and if they didn't have any ideas, I would come up with one. As long as their idea wasn't too extravagant, we'd do it. If they wanted to get pedicures, I was game. I needed to embrace the fact that my kids still liked hanging out with me. Going on a solo date night with me was exactly the connection they needed (especially with three other siblings), and it's only grown from there. Spending one-on-one time with them makes them feel as they should: like the most important thing in the world.

My Number One

We all have a specific love language that makes us feel special. My love language is a difficult one—it's acts of service. However, my wife Amanda's love language is quality time. There are different definitions of quality time depending on who you talk to. Amanda's version isn't just time together; it's being together and being present. Before I dig into this, let's look at it from a different angle.

Let's assume for a second that you have an important appointment on your calendar. What do you do to prepare? I assume you'll make sure every "T" is crossed and every "I" is dotted. You'll role-play the conversation, anticipate objections, and, to a degree, over-prepare. So why don't we prepare the same way for time with our top priorities? Normally, I would just show up or wing it.

I knew it was important to have a good date night strategy, but if I put thought into it and showed up present, it would deliver a message that Amanda was important and appreciated. Date nights with your spouse shouldn't rest on top of the "good intentions pile." It's easy to say we're too busy, or it's tough to find the time, but if it's a priority, you'll make the time. If you struggle like me to stay consistent, build it into your calendar. I would also ask your spouse how often they'd like to go on a date. Does date night always have to mean going to dinner? Does it always mean leaving the house? No. Sometimes, date night can be as simple as finding a new walking path and going for a walk. We've found that our most impactful date nights require very little financial investment—just being together and learning about each other is all we need.

Eliminate Distractions That Send the Wrong Message

We live in a very distracted world. When Amanda and I would go on dates, we'd observe how other couples spent time together— not to judge but to see what we didn't want in our own time together. We noticed that, at restaurants, many couples would be out together but not talking. They'd be scrolling on their phones. They were physically present but mentally elsewhere. When I'm with my wife or my kids, I ask myself, "What is so important that I need to be on my phone right now?" Absolutely nothing. I know that may sound judgmental, but let's put the phone down and connect with the person right in front of us. We don't know how much time we have together, so let's truly be together.

I challenge you to identify the number one distraction you have on your phone that offers you nothing in return and delete it. I found myself being addicted to a game. It came out of nowhere, but I was playing on my phone in my free time. For what purpose? My family was also found playing the same game, but once I deleted it from my phone, I noticed they stopped playing it as well. Delete that app right now, and give yourself at least one week away from it.

You Missed It

As parents, we're basically glorified Uber drivers. Using Kamryn as an example, she's a talented member of her competitive cheerleading program. On the way to practices, she'd tell me about the skill she was working on and how close she was to accomplishing it. I'd go into her practice and watch, and I absolutely loved when she landed a new skill and looked up to see if I was watching. I loved seeing her little toothless smile, full of joy. I knew this was important to her, and it was going to be a huge part of her life, so until I was kicked out during COVID, I made sure to watch. I could have easily been scrolling through social media or watching Netflix, but quality time isn't always about talking—it's also about being present while they focus on their priorities. I know phones and technology are addictive, and I fight that battle like everyone else, but our children are watching.

Prize Fighter Day

An incredible professional experience I was invited to attend was a financial advisor boot camp in 2014 hosted by a phenomenal leader named Ben Newman. If you don't know Ben Newman's content, get to know it quickly. Ben injects a great deal of motivation, drive, and ownership over your life into all attendees. One area we really focused on was developing what he calls a "Prize Fighter Day." Ben's strategy is to do one personal, one professional, and one random act of service every day. If done daily and stacked over time, this creates an unbelievable life with a massive amount of impact. My personal goal was to connect with at least one member of my family every day. This seemed like a small thing, but it made a huge impact on both me and my family.

I built it into my calendar to make a connection with someone daily. I started easy by connecting with Amanda, the kids, my sister, and my parents, but then the real impact came from connecting with the next layer of family. I built much stronger connections with grandparents, step-siblings, aunts, and uncles. I still remember the excitement in my grandparents' voices when I reached out. My grandma would yell at my grandpa, *"Hurry and pick up the phone—Dan's calling!"* We often underestimate our ability to brighten someone's day. This was only ten years ago, and since then, three of those family members I made a point to connect with have unfortunately passed away. I can honestly say I have no regrets. I'm thankful that we were able to connect on a deeper level.

I know I was just as responsible for the lost relationships as anyone. I was focused on providing for my family and growing my business. As you probably noticed, my last sentence was all about *me*. I wanted to connect with those around me because if they were gone tomorrow, I'd give anything in the world to have them back.

Action Items

1. RIGHT now, call one family member you have lost contact with and just catch up. Repeat once a day for a full week.

2. Find some conversation cards you can use with your children.

3. Recalibrate date night with your significant other.

4. Leave the phone in the vehicle at your child's next sporting event.

5. Shut the radio off the next time you are driving anywhere with your kids and talk to them, but ask open-ended questions.

CHAPTER 6

BOOK THE TRIP

This is one of the most important topics I wanted to make sure was included in the book. I want to discuss the concept of "*Book the Trip*." Book the Trip goes much deeper than literally booking a trip. It's about taking action on all the things you've wanted to do. It's about applying some of that Yes Man mentality and going for it. Would my wife describe me as impulsive? Of course she would. I am 100% emotional, I embrace taking risks, and I am very decisive when I make decisions. If the alternative is inaction, I'm okay with that. I do believe you can take calculated risks to live your life. That said, I have also made some poor choices due to my impulsiveness.

We recently took the Ferguson family trip to our current favorite getaway spot, a small community called Port St. Joe, Florida. We rent a VRBO that sits right on the beach. We make the 18-hour drive, like the Griswolds, all the way down to the 30A highway coastline. On the way home, I had my 15-year-old Kamryn, her good friend, and my 6-year-old Lucy in the car with me. The teenagers were sleeping, and I had a funny conversation with Lucy:

Lucy: Dad, how much money did it take to go on this trip?

Me: The trip wasn't cheap, but I had an amazing time.

Lucy: Was it $100?

Me: Lucy, all in, the trip was more than $11,000.

If you could have seen the look on her beautiful little face—it was priceless. Granted, she's 6 and doesn't fully grasp what a lot of money is.

Lucy: Are we going to go broke because of the trip and lose our house?

Me: Lucy, there's only one reason I would be okay with going broke: if the money is spent on having experiences with my family. I'd take that deal and be willing to go broke all day long.

I would rather die broke, living life and sharing experiences with my family, than die rich and full of regret.

I'm a certified financial planner, and I'm comfortable with my clients reading this and hearing me say I'd go broke by experiencing life with my kids. Why? Because I find so many people want to build unbelievable legacies to leave behind for the next generation, yet they lack the ability to enjoy the money they've accumulated by spending it on experiences with their kids. I believe we form our relationship with money as we enter our teenage years. The way we were raised and the experiences we did or didn't have shape the way we view money as we age.

My Childhood

I grew up in a small town called Falls City, Nebraska. My parents had my sister right out of high school, and I came along four short years later. My parents did the best they could to provide for my sister and me, but we weren't exactly touring the world as kids. Our vacations were spent driving to Denver to stay with my aunt and uncle. We got quality time during the 11-hour drive, which was disastrous at times. As a child growing up in the '80s and '90s, we had a cassette case, and our entertainment was waiting our turn to fast-forward to the song we wanted to hear. We would line up the cassettes and anticipate when our song was coming up. We also played car bingo and other games because we didn't have technology to pass the time.

My mom had the ability to double dip financially by using her PTO from her full-time job, and then she would work for my aunt, who ran a house-cleaning business. The adults would work during the day to generate some income to help fund the trip. I didn't know at the time that working on vacation was abnormal, but at least we were out of Nebraska. Once the parents were done for the day, we would enjoy some activities. We didn't spend every year on white sandy beaches or in mountain cabins, but you know what? We spent time together. I enjoyed that time, but I wanted my kids to experience family time along with new adventures.

As a mentor to younger advisors, they often ask me what I do when my business seems slow, and I start to feel stressed. My answer is simple: *I book a trip.* You should see the confusion on their faces.

They ask, "*Isn't that negligent?*" Absolutely, I tell them. But it wakes me up, lights my fire, and reconnects me with why I do what I do. My time with family is so important to me that I don't want my inability to perform at work to prevent me from doing the things I love. I understand that it seems backward to most, but I always want to have something to look forward to. If I find myself sitting stagnant and need a wake-up call, this is what I do, and it works every time.

Die With Zero

Once I decided to write this book and explained what I wanted to write about, I was told to read *Die With Zero*[4] by Bill Perkins. His message aligns with mine on so many levels. The book centers around the concept of dying with zero regrets but also dying with zero money. Now, it's almost a mathematical improbability to spend your last dollar the day you pass away. However, I don't personally want my kids hovering around my deathbed waiting for me to go because the potential wealth we're transferring to them will finally allow them to live their lives. I would much rather spend that money with them while we're alive and enjoy those experiences together. I don't want to wait until I'm 65 to begin living life when my body may not be as capable as it is now. By age 65, my kids may be older and no longer have the desire to join me, as their lives will be busier. I want to do the things we love now, and that doesn't mean we need to spend hundreds of thousands of dollars a year traveling the world.

---

[4] Perkins, Bill, *Die with Zero: Getting All You Can From Your Money And Your Life*. Boston: Mariner Books / Houghton Mifflin Harcourt, 2021.

It just means we need to invest in time together. I personally don't like spending money on materialistic items because I don't feel the need to impress anyone. When I see someone buy a $6,000 handbag, I see that as a week in Florida with my family. That doesn't mean we don't still enjoy nice things, but if it's a decision between a nice item or a family vacation—it's a no-brainer.

The Gift of a Memory

Amanda and I wanted to develop strategies that aligned with living life the way we wanted with our children. We decided to change how we purchased gifts for the kids as they grew older. Once they turn 10, we spend very little on gifts or technology. Instead, we invest in experiences—concerts, unique activities, new hobbies, or sporting events. I want to meet them at their level, but I also want them to meet me at mine. When we do that, we build a rich relationship together. Owen will laugh at this if he's reading, but when he was much younger, he was a huge Macklemore fan. For his birthday, we bought him tickets to a Macklemore concert. That meant Owen and I had an evening of hanging out, seeing a great performer, and creating a memory. Then it was my turn to show him a concert from my genre. I took him to see the Foo Fighters with Amanda and me. Owen will be a Foo Fighters fan for life now, not only because of that experience but because he saw the greatest rock band ever.

I mentioned earlier in the book that when you start making these investments with your family, weird things begin to happen.

It's almost like a higher power is tipping its hat to you. Here's what I mean: Owen has seen the Foo Fighters twice, once in Kansas City and once in Sioux Falls, SD. Both times, we met members of the band before the show. We didn't line up or pay for a meet-and-greet; we just happened to be in the right place at the right time. We've had so many of these kinds of moments that create lasting memories. I do feel it's a sign that someone is telling us we're doing the right things. The following are three photos of these moments.

Invest in those experiences, and don't tuck them away, waiting for the *perfect time*. If you keep putting off booking these experiences, before you know it, the time will be gone, and you'll be carrying around regret. I don't want anything I've said to be taken out of context—if I'm putting my family at risk by making certain decisions, that's a different story. The idea of spending time on experiences with your family still needs to be done with a certain level of planning.

I just feel like we live in a world where we're not as spontaneous as we should be. We overthink things, and we're afraid of change. Booking a family trip has become a mandatory thing that we do every year, but if there's an experience available in between these larger trips, I'm going to do what I can to make it happen. If you're sitting there thinking, *"We should take the kids to Disney World,"* book the damn trip—figure it out. However, remember what Pastor Josh said: the best relationships are those that always have something to look forward to. We apply this idea when we're on a trip. Normally, we'd feel that depressing sense of it coming to an end as we packed up to go home. Now, we just pull out the calendar and say, *"Where are we going next?"* My biggest hope in life is that my kids develop this mentality and spend their lives living. I want them to not only feel empowered to go for it but also to invest in doing life with the people they love.

Boundaries While Away

Being away from the office doesn't necessarily mean being away from work. At one point in time, I was afraid to leave because I'd just come home to more work without ever being able to fully disconnect. I was checking emails, returning quick calls, etc., and I know my family felt that my mind was in a different place. I know many people who struggle with this exact issue. How can you develop some level of separation from your business? Let me explain how we were able to address it.

My co-workers know that when we're taking family time away from work, they won't hear from me. We have a rule in our office, which took time to establish, that if I'm away with my family, please leave me be. In theory, that's the way it should be, but most of us are guilty of not being able to fully separate. I always tell them that if they have good news to share, by all means, reach out, but if it's negative or a "do you have a minute" situation, save it until I'm back. I don't want to be on a trip with my family and have it ruined by something that can be dealt with later. I've even gotten to the point where I delete my work email from my phone and leave my computer at the office to completely eliminate distractions. I know some clients or friends who go on family trips and work half the time—that's their choice. But that's not happening with this crew.

YOLO

There are many things we leave in the "I should" pile—things we really want to do but, for some reason, we hold back. There are usually three reasons we don't follow through on something: we don't know how, we don't want to, or we're scared to. Is fear holding us back? Take this book, for example. I held back for the longest time because I was scared of the commitment—the commitment of time and the commitment of money. At least, that's what I told myself and anyone who asked. But deep down, I know it was more because I thought, "*What if someone picks this book up and thinks it's worthless?*" That was nothing more than my ego getting in the way. I embrace humility well, but I was stuck in inaction. Finally, a friend of mine called and said, "I'm going to introduce you to Cris, who works for Game Changer Publishing, and it's time you write the book." I needed someone to take that first step for me. I hope to be that voice for someone else. I've come to terms with the fact that many people may not find this book fulfilling, but the people I care about will always have my words on paper, and I went for it.

Whether it's opening your own business, writing a book, calling someone to settle a grudge, booking the trip, or even getting a face tattoo—GO FOR IT.

Taking Action

I encourage you to stop right now and identify that one thing you keep procrastinating on and COMMIT! Find someone who will hold you accountable and tell them it's time for you to do it.

Anniston is our 13-year-old, and she has a strong outlet and passion for art. For her birthday, we bought her art lessons, which we thought would last for a few months. We are now going on five years, and it has hands down been the best investment we've made for her. Not only is she incredibly talented, but art is therapeutic for her in this high-stress world for teenagers. When Amanda and I want to connect with Anniston, we'll purchase paint-by-numbers because neither of us is anywhere near her talent level. We meet her on her level. I'm able to see the level of detail she puts into her art, and I know it makes her feel connected to us.

Attending her art class and seeing the quality of her work inspired me to do something most people would say is crazy. I have always wanted a half-sleeve tattoo, but I didn't have a clue what I wanted on my arm. I gave Anniston the concept of visually representing *"building my best life."* Anniston worked hard to bring the concept to life, and I gave her a high-level idea of what I wanted it to look like. On my 41st birthday, during a family vacation, she gave me her drawing, and it blew me away. It looked incredible, and she used her artistic mind to add her own ideas. I decided to take it to a tattoo artist and had them put it on my arm exactly as she drew it, initials and all. It has so much meaning to me, but I know it has a tremendous amount of meaning for her as well. I know to some, that's extreme, but there's nothing I love more than seeing that on my arm every day.

My Legacy

I want my legacy to be experiences with my family. I want my kids to look back on our time together and think of it as A+ time. I need to make the investment—I don't need to overthink things; I just need to make it happen. If they turn around and give that same treatment to their kids, and the pattern continues, that would be worth more than any financial legacy I could ever leave. If I go too soon in this life, I've planned fiscally to make sure they'll be taken care of. However, if I live a full life, I hope the bank will bounce the check the day I die.

Action Items

1. How does your childhood impact how you view money today?

   _____

   _____

   _____

   _____

   _____

   _____

2. What boundaries do you need to establish that can allow you to

   disconnect when you are away with your family?

   _____

   _____

   _____

   _____

   _____

3. What do you want your legacy to be? How do you want to be remembered?

_____

_____

_____

_____

_____

_____

4. Did you do the action item a few pages back? If not, what are you afraid of?

_____

_____

_____

_____

_____

_____

CHAPTER 7

POWER OF PERSPECTIVE

Perspective is your greatest superpower, or it can be your kryptonite. By itself, it can completely change how we view the world. I have struggled for much of my life with this mindset, and quite frankly, I still do. I felt like I grew up as a victim of my circumstances, almost operating as though I was owed something. It seemed like things just happened to me or my family, and we were the unlucky ones. My business coach, Tricia, identified something I had never seen in myself. She said, "*Dan, I absolutely have clients* with *a fear of failure, and I try to coach them through this. But you, my friend, have a fear of success. It seems like anytime things are going great, you self-sabotage.*" She couldn't have been more accurate. Anytime I started gaining momentum, I would dig myself back into a hole—whether by blowing money on ridiculous things, hurting a relationship, or losing all the good habits that had my business rolling. I just couldn't accept that I could be a victor in my circumstances and succeed. At that moment, I realized my biggest enemy was myself. I was either going to allow this victim mentality to dictate my future or learn about myself and take my narrative in a different direction.

Almost any situation we deal with can be seen differently depending on how we choose to see it. And it is a CHOICE. Some people see a glass half full, and others see it half empty. Either way, we still have half a glass, so neither is wrong. How I chose to see things made a massive impact on me professionally, personally, and, at times, financially. For some of us, it takes a tragic event to realize how good we have it. I want to use this chapter to walk through some stories and strategies that I believe could make a tremendous impact on how you view your life in general.

It Can Be the Smallest Event That Changes Your Life

In 2005, I was in my first year as an advisor. I had a day circled on my calendar for weeks, as I was finally going to wrap up business on my largest opportunity by far. I thought I'd finally catch up financially, get some much-needed breathing room, and prove to my family that I made the right career choice. My meeting was a two-and-a-half-hour drive away. The air felt clearer, the sun hit my skin better, the coffee tasted incredible, and the music sounded perfect all the way to my appointment. I arrived, greeted the secretary, and asked to see my client in a confident, positive tone. She reached out to let him know I was in the lobby.

After 25 minutes of waiting, she came back and told me he didn't have time to meet and was no longer interested in doing business with me. I won't go into more detail for confidentiality reasons, but my ego was checked. Instead of leaving with the compensation I'd counted on, I was left with nothing but lost time and out-of-pocket travel expenses. I put my tail between my legs and followed my MapQuest directions back to Lincoln. As I was driving back, I decided the ups and downs of client building weren't for me anymore. I was letting my business be run by my emotions instead of logic. I called my boss and told him I wasn't cut out for the business and that today was my last day. He told me he understood but suggested I sleep on it and we'd talk in the morning.

As I was driving through Omaha on my way to Lincoln, I looked up and saw the flashing lights of a police car behind me. *I can't catch a break*, I thought as the cop walked toward my car.

Police Officer: Do you know how fast you were going?

Me: No, sir, not exactly, but I know I was going well over the speed limit.

Police Officer: You were going 15 miles over the speed limit. Why are you in such a hurry?

Me: Honestly, I'm not in a hurry. I've had a rough day and got my teeth kicked in. I decided to quit my job, so I was speeding more out of frustration.

Police Officer: Hang tight while I run your information and bring you back the next steps to get you on your way.

My entire perspective on life changed in that instant. I thought to myself, *What I wouldn't give to go back just 20 minutes and slow down. If I had been traveling even just 8 MPH slower, I wouldn't be getting pulled over.* That's when it hit me. I thought I was having the worst professional day of my life and was ready to quit my job because things didn't go my way, yet I would give anything to go back to that moment and realize it wasn't so bad. I was feeling all these emotions over a $100 speeding ticket. A $100 speeding ticket is a pebble in the big scheme of life. However, it gave me the perspective to realize that things are never as bad as they seem, but they're also never as good as they seem either. The cop returned to my window and handed me a warning, saying, *"Cheer up and slow down. You've had a long enough day already."*

I felt like a baby, but I was grateful I got out of a decent-sized ticket. A part of me also felt like the entire series of events happened by design, like a higher power was giving me a reality check. Instead of wallowing in self-pity, I reframed my perspective and became productive the rest of the day. I used the drive home to focus on what I could control and started booking new appointments. I felt an insane pressure relief that motivated me to a new level. It was pure gratitude for a small life lesson that almost ended my career.

The next day, I showed up at work, and my boss said, *"I thought you were quitting."*

I replied, *"Not yet, brother. I haven't gotten my ass kicked enough yet."*

We are faced with opportunities to grow every day; they're just disguised as challenges.

Ego Check

In 2018, I went through a significant professional challenge. I was doing everything in my power to keep perspective front and center, but I knew I needed guidance. I had gone through a rough patch that year and reached out to Pastor Josh for advice. I explained how I had to let go of my best advisor and one of my best friends. Losing someone with that level of influence created a lot of doubt in the office. We had issues with our culture, our administrative team needed improvements, and many veteran advisors lost confidence and made career changes. In the words of Jim Carrey in *Dumb and Dumber*, "Our pets' heads were falling off."[5]

We went from being the most dominant office in the state to the lowest-performing in less than three months. I was maxed out with stress. I reached out to Josh, and we had coffee. As always, he asked clarifying questions and took some time to think. I was waiting for him to give me advice on how to rebuild our culture and get back on track. Instead, he completely changed the subject.

Josh: Can I ask your advice on something?

Me: Of course.

Josh: At the end of every church service, I pray for those in our government and law enforcement, asking that they continue to protect and guide us.

---

[5] Farrelly, Peter, director. *Dumb and Dumber.* New Line Home Entertainment, 1997.

He paused for a moment.

Josh: Every week after the service, I get a message from a few people in the congregation. They send me scathing emails, telling me I need to stop praying for President Donald Trump. What do you think about that, Dan?

At first, I thought, *Is he being serious right now?* Here I was, explaining how my business was losing money, my culture was falling apart, and he was worried about a few emails? So I said:

Me: Something like that wouldn't bother me. I'd just brush it off and move on.

Josh: Yeah, I figured you'd say that. But Dan, I lose sleep two nights a week over it. I feel like I'm letting everyone in the church down. I really struggle with this issue.

I was shocked by his response, but then he put it into perspective. He said, "*We all believe what we're experiencing is the biggest thing going on in the world. From the outside looking in, your problem seems easy to solve. Yet our problems are always bigger than everyone else's, and they become even bigger when we try to control what we can't control.*"

We are in control of our problems, but we need to focus on controlling what we can, not what we can't. Also, we all feel our issues are larger than everyone else's, but the more we try to control what we can't, the worse things get. We needed clarity on where we were going as an office, a strategy to make it possible, and accountability to believe in ourselves. Every person we lost and every dollar that blew away blessed us with the collateral beauty of what we were building. This was just another warning that our minds were feeding the wrong wolf. We needed to be victors, not victims of our circumstances, and control the controllables. As easy as this is to write, it can feel like an impossible feat to overcome.

The Greatest Hire

When the business was crumbling, we needed to make improvements. I had received the feedback I needed to receive, but I was still slow to take action. A few weeks after talking to Pastor Josh, I was at a directors' conference with my family. It was at Paradise Island in the Bahamas. I was literally in paradise with the family, trying to just enjoy the trip, and our office manager texted me saying she was not coming back after maternity leave. *Can I catch a break?* Sound familiar? With all the stress I was feeling, I couldn't sleep, so the next morning I was up walking around the resort at five in the morning; I was trying to figure out how to work out of this mess that was happening. At this time of the morning, at a resort, the only people awake were the staff preparing the outdoor areas and me. As I was walking back into the property to grab a cup of coffee, I ran into my favorite motivational speaker of all time, INKY JOHNSON. He turned a tragedy into triumph! I could not believe my eyes. I stopped him right before he took off on his morning run:

Me: Ink, man, I feel I was meant to run into you today. I am going through a very tough moment in my business, and I don't see a way out.

Inky: Man, everything happens for a reason. You'll be alright. Just hang in there and keep the faith.

Me: I appreciate it, man. No one will believe me, so can I please grab a photo? This was meant to happen.

Inky: Of course.

It was a short interaction that made a lifelong impact. I was falling back into a victim mindset, and I needed to stop dwelling on what I couldn't control and start focusing on what I could. I needed to bring someone onto the team who I trusted and who I knew would work hard. I had Tricia holding me accountable to my vision and Amanda holding me accountable at home, but I needed someone in the office to keep me focused. I made a bold move and hired my sister away from her career in Lincoln to join us in Omaha right after I grabbed my coffee.

Erica was on this trip with us to help with the kids when I was at leadership sessions. She had no background in the business, but I trusted her with anything in the world. From day one, she treated the business like it was her own and was laser-focused on building a strong culture with great efficiency. I was initially hesitant about hiring family, but seeing them every day and knowing their salary depended on my performance kept me extremely focused. I don't think my sister, Erica, will ever know the full impact she had on our business and the light she brings into the office every day, but I can confidently say none of us would be where we are without her help.

Putting This Perspective into Others

Whenever someone close to me goes through a major life event, like a divorce, loss of a family member, or job loss, and asks for my thoughts, I always respond the same way: "Sit back and enjoy the collateral beauty that comes from this." It's hard to see beauty in the moment of challenge, but the largest growth we experience as humans often happens during adversity. I choose not to lean in with sympathy but to challenge them to see the growth they're experiencing and embrace it.

Words Matter

Whether I'm coaching seventh-grade girls' basketball or talking to clients, colleagues, or family, I explain how words matter. I don't have to do anything. I get to do these things. We are so blessed with the world we wake up to every day, and so many people would give anything to be where we are. Referring back to the Yes Man mentality with my kids, there are many people unable to have children, or worse, some who have lost a child. And here I am, potentially complaining because my kids want to play with me? I don't have to do anything with my kids—I get to do these things. I don't have to respond to a client email or pick up the phone to schedule a new client—I get to do these things.

Action Item: I challenge you to correct yourself over the next 48 hours every time you say "HAVE TO" and change it to "GET TO." Try to count how many times you correct yourself in that period.

The Teacher Learns as Much as the Student

My final thought on framing your perspective is by far the most powerful one. How can you just live in your priority and not sit there as a shell of yourself, coasting through the motions while thinking of something else? This is much harder than people think, and we hate to admit it. I struggled with this for a long time, but I've finally found a way to truly live in the moment.

During our Ferguson family vacation in Port St. Joe, Florida, we had a few moments where we experienced a perspective shift. I mentioned in previous chapters that when I book a trip and go away, I have principles and rules that my office knows about. Number one, I delete my work email, and I need a code to reinstall it. They're not allowed to reach out with normal tasks. If I'm gone, I don't want anyone reaching out to me with, "Hey, do you have a moment?" or "Hey, something bad happened." I'll deal with that when I'm back. I don't want to sit on a trip with my family, feeling like I need to unplug from them and plug back into work. It's extremely healthy to disconnect, and it makes me so much more productive when I return refreshed. I don't want my identity to be wrapped up in not being present during these important moments. There were a few moments on the trip that helped us truly CONNECT to the moment we were in, and I wanted to share them.

Amanda and I decided to divide and conquer our 18-hour trek down to Port St. Joe, so we had to split into two vehicles. On the way down, I was blessed with three teenage girls: our 13-year-old Anniston, 15-year-old Kamryn, and Kamryn's best friend. The four of us hopped in the truck, which was loaded with drinks, snacks, and pillows. I started the journey by plugging in the address, and the screen showed 1,189 miles to our destination. No matter what age you are, seeing that makes you tired. Call this clichéd, but whenever I feel the energy shift to the negative, I remind the girls, "*One week from now, you'll give anything in the world to be at the front end of this trip, so let's embrace this moment.*" Oddly, even for teenagers, it helped flip their energy and their perspective on the drive. We played a game to see how many state license plates we could identify, used conversation cards, and blasted our favorite songs. It made the entire trip smoother because I know with confidence that having this perspective allows them to appreciate the journey.

On our third day, Amanda and I were sitting by the pool while the kids were making s'mores together. Of course, the older kids were giving our 6-year-old Lucy a hard time. We were about to jump in and tell them to leave her alone, but instead, I looked at Amanda and said, "*Next week around this time, I'll probably be in a meeting I don't want to be in, thinking to myself what I wouldn't give to be in this exact moment right now.*" Amanda looked at me and said, "*Can you just enjoy it while we're here?*" She wasn't wrong, but I told her, "*That's how I enjoy the moment—I realize how much I'll want to come back to this exact moment one week from now.*" It helps me disconnect from the chaos of normal life and soak up every moment while I'm there. I don't want short-term distractions to ruin a lifelong memory. In most situations, I use the future as fuel to get through tough times, but in return, I want to steal the emotion of wanting to be back on vacation to lock into the moment we're in.

Finally, there was one moment that was more powerful than all the others. Up to this point, you might be thinking these are just feel-good moments, but I can confidently say that the power of a positive perspective can change how everything looks through your lens. It was now our last day at Port St. Joe. The kids were slow to get up after staying up too late crab hunting the night before. Amanda and I used the quiet time in the morning to game plan for the drive home and figure out what we needed to pack. Isn't that last day just the worst feeling? After eight days of being disconnected, we could feel all the stressors coming back. We had 1,189 miles of driving the next day. I could see all the kids start to mope around, and I felt it in my own stomach. As a parent, you hate to see the energy drain out of your family.

At that moment, I was sitting waist-deep in the pool next to the house. I yelled to the kids, "*Hey, everybody, come down here real quick. I have something I want to talk to you about.*" They came down the stairs with that look that said, "Dad's going to tell us what we need to pack up for the drive home." I told all five kids to sit down in the chairs by the pool for a moment.

Me: *I want everyone to close your eyes for me.*

And, of course, they kept one eye open, thinking I was going to pull them into the pool or something.

Me: *No, I'm not going to pull you into the pool, but please close your eyes. What I want you to imagine is that it's December 3rd. It's starting to get dark by 5:30, the wind is blowing snow sideways, and when you walk outside, it pierces your face and burns your skin because it's a windchill of -10 in Nebraska. There's salt all over the house from the road crews, and you feel dirty all the time. All you want to do is hide under blankets. It's miserable.*

I saw all their faces start to cringe.

Me: Do you feel it? Now, imagine a portal opens and transports you right back to Port St. Joe, Florida, on the front porch of our VRBO. The weather is 90 degrees, just like it is right now, and you're given 10 minutes before you're sent back to Nebraska. My question is: what would you do with your time?

Without exception, all of them said they'd run to the beach, feel the heat under their feet, and dive into the ocean. I said, "*You can open your eyes, but I want you to realize you're acting like you've already been teleported back to December 3rd. Instead of having 10 minutes, you have 10 hours left before we go to sleep.*" They looked at each other, smiled, and ran to put on their swimsuits before diving into the ocean.

After injecting this energy back into our trip, amazing things started happening the rest of the day. The people sitting next to us had been fishing the entire trip. They asked the girls if they wanted to fish, and the girls were elated. They ended up catching a stingray and some other fish.

Lucy was able to connect for one last day with the friends she made on the trip, and they had their best pool day yet. However, the most amazing part came at the end of the sunset. Amanda, Anniston, and I were hitting the volleyball around on the beach as the sun was setting. Anniston hit the ball over my head, and it was heading toward the ocean. When I picked it up, I looked down the coastline, and my eyes could not comprehend what I was seeing. I tried to yell for Amanda and Anniston, but I just took off running, and they followed. Crawling on the beach was an enormous sea turtle. She was either coming ashore to lay eggs or checking on her nest. We spoke to many locals, and most had never seen a sea turtle on land—it was an incredible moment. We almost missed all these amazing experiences because of a negative perspective. So, the next time you're on a trip and feel the "end of the trip blues" setting in, just reframe your thinking—it may turn into a day that lives in your core memories forever.

The next day, as we were heading home, I asked the kids, "What did you learn on this trip?"

They said, "I need to learn to change my perspective and just enjoy the moments that I'm in."

To me, that was the best feeling in the world—to hear them start seeing the world that way. I can only pray they continue to reframe their environment. I would love for my legacy to be a positive perspective rather than a large inheritance, any day of the week.

Reader's Reflection

- What has been the hardest adversity you have ever gone through? Looking back now, how did it change who you are today?

_____

_____

_____

_____

_____

_____

- Have almost given up on something that ended up working out?

_____

_____

_____

_____

_____

- What movie has the greatest comeback story of all time?

_____

_____

_____

_____

_____

_____

_____

CHAPTER 8

WORK IS FUEL

So far, I have spent most of the book identifying how to develop the system and mindset to be present at home. I also knew I needed to find a way to *lock* in when I was at work. Work/Life/Balance is frequently talked about, but for me to be at my best, I need structure and boundaries around each area. There's work life, and there's family life. Sadly, those lines can get blurred because we spend almost as much time—if not more—with our work family than we do with our own. Where it becomes unhealthy is when we take work home with us or bring our personal life into work. To me, that means robbing from both sides. If I can be good at my career and stick to my boundaries, I will *thrive* at home.

Every time I say yes to something professionally, I'm saying no to something at home. Seeing this has given me the ability to focus on my day-to-day obligations, but when the work is done and it becomes an option, I go home to my top priority. I've worked hard to create strong boundaries regarding how I use my time during the workday. I'm aware that in my role, I'll be asked to go on retreats, company trips, developmental trainings, and attend client appointments at non-traditional times. If I can trade time for time instead of time for money, it relieves any guilt I may feel. My vision, combined with my ideal calendar, became the two most important tools for establishing firm boundaries. Let's dig in deeper.

Importance of Energy Control

I added another layer of strategy that really increased my productivity. I built my ideal calendar to follow my emotional schedule. Your emotional schedule is about identifying your top energy points and how each day affects you. I figured everyone felt the same energy as me. I am very productive professionally on Monday, Tuesday, and Wednesday, especially in the mornings. Similar to eating food, I eat what I don't like first so I can enjoy the rest of the meal. I built my schedule the same way—I wanted as many meetings as possible earlier in the week rather than later. I learned that having appointments that didn't give me much energy on a Friday dragged me down all week.

Not everyone has full control of their schedule, and I totally understand that. For me, trading time for time means I'm okay working longer hours on a Monday, even taking a few client meetings until 7 PM. However, if I do that, I take Friday afternoon off to balance it out. It's not aligned with my vision or energy to load up on work throughout the week. My career fuels the life I want, and while I care deeply about my clients, advisors, and leadership team, they respect that I have my priorities straight. I encourage you to do an internal inventory of your energy and identify patterns when you're at your best, then build your business around that. I asked a few other co-workers what their favorite day of the week was to pack their schedules, and I went 3 for 3 with us all having an entirely different day. Mine was Tuesday, another said Wednesday, and one said Friday.

Creative Avoidance and Distraction

When I operated as a workaholic, I felt exhausted all the time. I felt like I was working 100-hour weeks. When I realized I was operating like an iPhone, I knew something was broken. Some days, I was just "playing office"; present, but there was no clear measure of a successful day. I would have spent my time doing tasks that were unproductive in nature but which kept me busy, also known as "creative avoidance": the meaningless tasks we decide to do instead of focusing on profitable tasks. I would grab coffee refills, stop by people's desks to talk, do $15/hour work that wasn't my job, etc. I would spend my time doing anything to avoid the much more difficult work, the work that takes you out of your comfort zone. There's no growth in the comfort zone.

On days filled with creative avoidance, I'd go home thinking about the things I didn't do. Once I became more efficient, I found myself leaving the office earlier and being more productive. I started focusing on my inputs—what I was putting into the day—rather than the outputs or results. If I followed my principles, I would have gone home and not taken work home with me. I began to utilize my top priority by holding it hostage to perform at a more elite level. I would put in measurable metrics like *"I won't go home until I have been referred to five new potential clients,"* and I would be held accountable by my coach. That's a small way to connect the right and left sides of my brain. The left side of my brain was telling me to get the referrals, but the right side of my brain wanted to go home. I saw others using similar tactics.

What Did They Think?

I also wanted to understand how I was showing up for the people around me. I did a 360-degree review, asking family, team members, and mentors what I was doing right and where I could improve. Amanda told me, *"If I could change anything, it would be great if you didn't come home from work still on your phone."* What's interesting about this is that whenever I bring it up in a group setting, people always say, "Oh, I hate it when my spouse comes home on their phone." Through this feedback, I realized that it made Amanda feel unimportant. It's a simple ask, but it was a habit I needed to really focus on. I told Amanda that I was going to fix this, though I wouldn't be perfect. I was comfortable with her calling me out when I slipped. I kept discovering that some of the smallest things sent the wrong message and needed boundaries.

I didn't stop there—I wanted to learn more. Was it okay for me to make a call or answer if an advisor needed me while I was at home? Amanda understood that I had clients and advisors who relied on me at inconvenient times. We both concluded that returning business calls at home was fine, but I needed boundaries. Like most people in leadership, I often get, "Hey, do you have a minute for a call?" We all know it's never just a minute, but I also don't like leaving advisors feeling unsupported. I'm a people pleaser, after all. My new response is simple: "I'm with the family right now. If it's urgent, I'll make the time, but if it can wait until tomorrow, that would be better." As you can guess, most calls can wait.

But what if it's urgent? Do I drop everything and call? To respect my family, I try to kill two birds with one stone. I take the dogs for a walk or run an errand I already had planned, and I return the call while I'm out. I don't want my family to always see me on my phone—it sends the wrong message. With the right boundaries, it can be managed.

BUILD IT

In my leadership role, I help advisors build their best life. I'm not a fan of the phrase "Live your best life." I believe you need to *build* it. When advisors start their careers, they have all this energy and excitement about creating their work life and taking control. But in my 17 years of leadership, I've seen that it doesn't take long for them to fall into patterns of "creative avoidance" and become like an iPhone running low on battery. Our advisors track their activity day to day, and it's interesting that when I coach advisors with low activity, they always seem the most worn down. They tell me they feel like they work all the time, but it's because they spend 90% of their time thinking about everything they didn't do, and they bring that stress home with them. It makes them irritable and stressed, and they begin to resent themselves for not channeling that energy in a positive way.

When this happens, I apply the strategies I've outlined to help them recalibrate their business. Just like machines, we need recalibration as humans when we start feeling stagnant. We need new energy and focus. However, it always comes back to the same conclusion: we need boundaries, clarity, and a strong focus on what's within our control. One of the hardest things to manage is what goes on between our ears. When we lack clarity about what we're working toward, it's hard to stay focused.

Let's use health as an example. If I asked any trainer for three to four things I could do within my control to get into better shape, they'd say it's easy: drink at least half your body weight in ounces of water daily, eat for fuel rather than pleasure, get 7–8 hours of sleep, and work out 4–5 times a week. The problem is that emotions often get in the way. If I followed this plan for two weeks and looked in the mirror, would I see amazing results? Probably not, and that's when my emotions would take over, pulling me back to old habits. Why is this the case with most things? Why do our emotions lead us in the wrong direction? It's because emotions focus on what feels good now, and they are over seven times more powerful than logic.

Habits are hard to build and easy to break while trying to build them. To create effective follow-through, I need clarity on what I want, a system to make it sustainable, and accountability. It takes doing something 30-60 days in a row to form a habit. Here's an example of how I applied this to a simple situation.

When I was in college, I had a hard time waking up early in the morning. I was bartending at night, taking 16 credit hours, raising my son Owen, and working an internship. It felt like fitting it all in was going to be almost impossible. I needed to find a way to make it work. So, I bought a second alarm clock. I set it to go off five minutes after the one in my room. The difference was that I placed the second alarm clock in Owen's room. When my alarm went off, my emotions would tell me to hit snooze, but my logic would tell me to wake up. Before I could fall back asleep, my emotions kicked in again: "Oh crap, I need to turn off Owen's alarm before it wakes up my screaming 1-year-old." I think you get the point: my emotions and logic connected, and I got up.

This strategy lasted about a month before waking up early became a habit. Everything I learned about these techniques was from the book *Following Through* by Steve Levinson & Pete Greider.[6] It is absolutely fantastic. The book identifies seven different ways of being able to follow through on commitments, and all of it is centered around connecting the left and right sides of your brain.

I realize I have frequently mentioned connecting the brain, but it's critically important to understand how to connect emotion with logic and the power that connection holds. As parents, we use this

---

[6] Levinson, Steve, and Pete Greider. *Following Through: A Revolutionary New Model for Finishing Whatever You Start.* Unlimited Publishing, 2015.

technique all the time with our children: "If you want Jane to spend the night this weekend, you'll need to clean your room." This book helped me better understand myself and how I follow through. I'm more motivated by the stick than the carrot—I tend to follow through when I have something to lose rather than when there's a reward at the end.

Pre-flight and Post-flight Routine

I know for sure that if I want something done and done right, I need to find a list-taker. I've challenged my advisors over time to apply this technique in their personal lives. I tell them to spend 30 minutes on a Friday morning identifying all the things they'd like to accomplish over the weekend—anything from calling a family member, scheduling a dog sitter, or mowing the yard. Once they have a solid list, I advise them to put it away for the rest of Friday. However, when Saturday comes, I suggest they put on jeans instead of sweats and see what happens. By setting the environment up for success (since no one likes sitting around in jeans), they'll be more motivated to start crossing things off the list and work until everything is done.

Why am I discussing this in the context of being efficient at work? From a work standpoint, creating a similar structure that you repeat daily can lead to monumental change and a much higher level of focus. I want to dig into this because, if implemented, it can change everything professionally. I call it my pre-flight and post-flight routine. I wanted to create a morning routine that felt as habitual as brushing my teeth—something I would feel lost without. Once I established a clear daily strategy to "win the day," it eliminated time spent on creative avoidance. More importantly, my post-flight routine is how I end my day. If I do this right, I'm able to stop taking work home with me.

I also wanted to change up my workout routine to get uncomfortable, so I started attending a hot yoga class in the mornings—and I absolutely love it. In yoga, they ask you to set your intention for the class, to release emotions or mental clutter that's consuming your thoughts. I wanted to apply the same idea professionally. I designed my pre-flight routine, which takes about 20–30 minutes each morning. The first thing I do is a quick financial update. I budget down to the penny and like to know exactly where I stand financially. This helps me recalibrate my thinking and start fresh—yes, I'm a bit of a numbers nerd. The second thing I do is review my schedule for the day and check to ensure my team, or I have uploaded everything needed for each case. Third, I go through any emails or texts left from the previous day that need reviewing or responses. Lastly, I assign any new tasks to my team and create a list of controllable tasks for myself to complete. I measure myself only by what I can control—not by the outcomes of the day or what my clients or colleagues may or may not accomplish. The clearer I am about my commitments for the day, the better I perform.

Of course, I still get positive or negative energy based on my daily results. I'm human, after all. But I've learned not to measure my sense of accomplishment by whether others say yes or no. For example, let's say my commitments for the day include calling or reaching out to 30 people, getting referred to three new individuals, completing an online assessment, and submitting paperwork to get licensed in another state. These are just hypotheticals. Now, it's 2:30 p.m., and I've accomplished all these tasks, with one last big meeting scheduled for 3 p.m. But then the client cancels, says they're no longer interested, and chooses to go in a different direction. Ouch! As a newer professional, that would have ruined my day. My insecurities would've flared up, and I would have worked even harder to try and make up for the lost client, coming home late and stressed.

But after adopting the mindset of controlling the controllables, I've learned that as long as I complete my commitments, I can head home feeling accomplished—even when things don't go perfectly. This mindset shift has drastically reduced my stress and has increased my productivity. Focusing more on inputs compared to outputs is a recipe for success.

My post-flight routine is by far the most important part of my day professionally. It's what allows me to go home and be fully present with my family rather than distracted by work. I used to hate the days when I'd spend all night thinking about work, itching to check my email, or waking up at 2 a.m. with my to-do list racing through my mind. This routine is simple, but for some, it might require a financial commitment. I want to be clear: I'm not promoting any specific service, but I want to explain my process in detail.

As soon as I pack up for the day and get in my truck to drive home, I immediately switch into wrap-up mode. When I start the truck, I call a dictation service called Copytalk, which many financial advisors know about. There are other services like this, but the key is that I use it to dictate all the notes and to-do items I've collected throughout the day. I dictate conversations I've had and any action items that need attention. Then, Copytalk transcribes everything into separate emails and sends them directly to my team. By the next morning, my team is already chipping away at those tasks, whether it's client requests, scheduling calls, or clarifying details.

This process has drastically reduced my need to constantly check my phone. In a way, I feel like my iPhone is in "do not disturb" mode, plugged in and recharging.

Implementing this strategy has been a game changer for me, and anyone already doing it would agree wholeheartedly. After completing my post-flight routine, if there are any urgent calls I need to make, I handle them before I get out of the car—even if that means circling the neighborhood a couple of times. This way, I can shut down the workday and recharge without bringing distractions into my home.

Nothing Good Happens at Night Professionally

"What if a client messages you and NEEDS to talk to you? Or what if I check my work email and feel compelled to respond?" I get this question a lot from advisors. My response would be, *"Who are you worried about letting down?"* First off, nothing good really ever

happens after 6 o'clock at night! Most clients prefer to email bad news at night, assuming you are gone for the day and hoping to avoid the conflict. I stay off my email almost 100% when I'm away. Did you see I used the word *almost* there? Yes, I am human, and every once in a while, I have a lapse of judgment. My intention is still good, but my judgment can be poor. I found that checking an email that has bad news robs you of the rest of your night. You're out of the office and can't do much about it, yet all your apps keep opening and creating a restless night. That's not fair to my top priority.

Action Items

1. Ask the closest people around you what you need to work on to be more present. Identify techniques to follow through on changes by connecting the right and left sides of your brain.

_____

_____

_____

_____

_____

2. Identify things you can do every morning that would help you cut the noise and focus on your day.

_____

_____

_____

_____

_____

3. Identify items that would help you leave work at work.

_____

_____

_____

_____

_____

_____

CHAPTER 9

GRATITUDE

From 1982 to 2014, I was pretty selfish and spent most of my time focusing on myself. That doesn't mean I lacked manners or was rude to everyone around me, but I was quite preoccupied with my own experiences. It would be a disservice not to discuss the power of gratitude, though. Gratitude was something I was lacking for a large majority of my life. Gratitude can be expressed in various ways, and life is undeniably hard.

Sadly, most people carry burdens they cannot let go of. Those burdens can fester inside of us and eliminate our ability to be grateful or appreciative of the life we have. Gratitude can be as simple as exchanging positive energy with someone else. I wanted my top priority to be the best version of myself. I also wanted to show up well for my clients, colleagues, and friends. As I found more energy to give back to others, I also wanted to bring a little light back into the world. As I mentioned in the last chapter, when I became more focused at home, I became more productive at work. Now that I'm no longer mentally draining myself by being in two places at once, I've gained even more energy—and I want to spread that to others.

Energy Exchange

Jon Gordon wrote *The Energy Bus*,[7] a tremendous book about making sure you have the right people on your "bus." He also addresses the concept of energy vampires. We all have them in our lives, and unfortunately, some are hard to avoid. You can almost feel the negativity coming off them, and you know that any conversation will revolve around how they've been wronged or how hard their life is. Some people are rarely exposed to positive energy, and if I can be that person for them, I would be honored.

Energy is absolutely infectious, and I've noticed we tend to mirror the people around us. Body language makes up 80% or more of our communication. If you find yourself in a conversation with someone who leans back, crosses their arms, and isn't paying attention, you'll likely do the same. Knowing that energy is contagious, I realized that I was losing the battle if I allowed myself to be brought down by others. If someone is on autopilot, walking around like a zombie, just going through the motions, it's up to me to stay in my energy and do my best to influence theirs.

I believe the world is simply exhausted. We are constantly distracted by misinformation, conflicted about where we should be, and, sadly, disappointed in ourselves—often full of insecurity. I've

---

[7] Gordon, Jon. 2007. *The Energy Bus*. Chichester, England: John Wiley & Sons.

been there, and sometimes, those feelings creep back in. Just think about this: when you walk into a room and ask someone a simple question like, "Hey, how's it going?" you'll either get a sarcastic remark or hear some complaint about how busy they are. What's worse is when you mirror their response and say, "Me too," because, in their mind, it diminishes how they feel. Everyone thinks they are busier than everyone else, and it becomes a competition of who works harder. Being busy has become a badge of honor, as people often equate busyness with productivity.

I wanted to begin changing my mindset and how I approached conversations. I started by bringing a smile and high energy into every room I entered. Even if I wasn't in the most positive headspace, my energy still impacted others to some degree—because if I smiled, they smiled. If I could get people to mirror me instead of the other way around, that would be powerful. Have you ever been around that annoyingly positive person who's always high energy and uses a high-pitched voice like, *"Hey, buddy, how are you doing?"* And you can't help but hug them back? That's an energy exchange I feel I can offer to many people—though maybe without the high-pitched voice!

What started happening was impactful: people began telling me that my energy was infectious and that I actually boosted their energy levels. What an amazing gift to give someone. I encourage you to spread high energy and an infectious smile for just one day and see how it changes your conversations. It will take some effort at first because you'll naturally fall back into old habits of mirroring the lowest energy around you, but the results are worth it.

Validate Them

As I mentioned earlier, Pastor Josh told me that some members of his church were unhappy with him for praying for the president. At the time, it didn't seem like a big deal to me, but for him, it meant everything. I'm not naive—I know people have bad days. Even though I try to counter their bad day with positive energy, I don't want to completely dismiss their experience. I also don't want to diminish their bad day by trying to "top" it with my own challenges. If someone needed someone to talk to, I wanted to lean into whatever they were going through and give them the space to get it off their chest. If they trusted me enough to share, I just wanted to listen. If they asked for my opinion, I'd give it, but I never wanted to devalue their pain.

There's so much impact in simply listening. But there's a big difference between hearing and listening. Hearing is when you're already formulating what you're going to say next while they're still talking—something I've been guilty of, like many others. This style of communication keeps things surface-level. True listening requires removing yourself from the equation, and honestly, it would take another entire book to address how to develop this skill. If you want to challenge yourself, the next time someone leans on you to listen, just listen. If you feel the urge to interject or start forming a response, try to control those thoughts and refocus on the person in front of you. It will deepen your relationship in ways you can't imagine.

I Appreciate You

Another level of expressing gratitude is thanking someone for their actions or words. This, too, is like a muscle that needs to be worked on. The first step is identifying people who've done something for you recently, those who've made a big impact in the past, or people you simply enjoy doing life with. The second step for me was to implement a strategy. So, I ordered a box of thank-you cards. Yes, they looked like the cards you send out after a wedding, but I didn't care about appearances—I just needed something to write on to express my gratitude. At first, I sent them to a few individuals who fit the criteria above: old mentors, clients who referred me to others, colleagues who believed in me, etc.

The energy boost I got from just writing and sending those cards was incredible. I couldn't wait for them to be read, though I wondered if it was more about me than them. I hated that I even had those thoughts. I had to rethink my motivations, but then I got a call from someone who said my letter had made their entire year. I asked why it meant so much to them. Sadly, they had been a coach and mentor for a long time, but after retiring, they felt forgotten. They said every thank you they'd received along the way seemed superficial. But knowing that someone who didn't stand to gain anything had taken the time to write a heartfelt, handwritten note made every moment they spent coaching worth it. That moment affirmed for me that it's okay to feel good about making an impact like this. I had a mental block about it, but receiving that message gave me the strength to move mountains. Thanking someone for an immediate action—like opening a door—is respectful. But letting someone know, unsolicited and unexpectedly, that they helped you get to where you are is one of the greatest gifts you can give.

Pay It Forward

"Keep calm and chive on" was a statement that rocked the world for a while. The absolute best part of that wild company was its commitment to paying it forward. Does expressing gratitude have a ripple effect? I truly believe it does. I was hopeful that anyone who received unsolicited gratitude would pay it forward, and that's the ripple effect I wanted to create. When I'd hear that someone paid it forward, it felt like I'd given $1 away and received $2 in return. And now I had $2 to give away, and I'd get back $4, and it kept compounding. People would say, "You know, that letter you sent meant a lot to me. I've kept it." Hearing that meant a lot to me, too. We live in a world where we feel like we're owed something by everyone all the time. It's normal, but I guess I wanted to be abnormal.

If you've read *The Five Love Languages*, you'll already know your own love language. Mine is the absolute worst: acts of service. If your love language is acts of service, you love having things done for you without having to ask. It makes me feel like Jennifer Aniston in *The Break-Up*: "I want you to want to do the dishes!"[8] That's me, and I feel sorry for everyone around me. Now, why is that a bad thing? Unfortunately, we tend to show love through our own love language. I'll do random things for people because I know they'll appreciate it, but if your love language is words of affirmation and you give me compliments, it won't do much for me in terms of feeling appreciated. It took me a long time to work through the fact that if I did something for someone, it was because I appreciated them—and if they didn't respond with over-the-top gratitude, that was okay. I no longer do things expecting anything in return. There's a dopamine hit in the brain when someone expresses gratitude, and it can make them more productive or inspire them to give back to someone else. Acts of gratitude can start with a simple text, phone call, or letter—anything to show respect. I can confidently say that taking the time to write a note means so much more than sending a text.

A Stranger Is a Friend Waiting to Happen

Putting positive energy into the world when interacting with complete strangers is one of the best things you can do. I'm very fortunate to live in "Nebraska Nice," which is, as they say, God's country. Sure, we don't have beaches or mountains, but I truly love where I live. In Nebraska, it seems like there are two main things people love to talk about: Husker football and the weather. I don't know why, but whenever I'd get on an elevator with a random

---

[8] Reed, Peyton director, *The Break-Up*. RBA, 2007.

stranger, and there was that awkward tension, I'd always end up saying something like, "It sure is cold out there today," or "Lost another close one." Of course, they would respond politely, but it always felt like an empty conversation.

I wanted to change that narrative. I started asking open-ended questions as if we had known each other forever. For example, instead of commenting on the weather, I'd say, "What are you most excited for this weekend?" You'd be surprised at how much this catches people off guard—it's actually pretty entertaining. Asking questions that encouraged upbeat conversation started cracking a few smiles. It's amazing how you can almost see their expression change from zombie-like to upbeat. I could be the most positive interaction they had all day.

Bringing that kind of energy kept me sharp and feeling good. I've even created some great friendships through this approach in places I frequent, like the grocery store or church. This might sound like a simple suggestion, but try it. Next time you're in a situation where you're almost forced to interact with someone you don't know, bring the energy. Sometimes it's as simple as stopping to thank a security guard for what they do.

Here's a quick example: Amanda and I were grocery shopping one day, and there was a young guy helping customers sign up for the store's membership rewards program. Amanda went to the produce section, and I walked past the guy, who said, "*Have a nice day*," like he probably did to everyone. I walked right by without saying a word, but then I stopped, turned around, and said, "*Brother, you just told me to have a nice day, and not only did I not reciprocate, I didn't even respond. I apologize. I'm having a great day, and I appreciate you. Do you have big weekend plans?"* He then told me about his weekend, but at the end, he said, *"Thanks for stopping, man. You just made my entire day."*

More importantly, my kids saw that. They started to see how you should treat people. My son Owen, who is 22, is a great kid. Throughout high school and college, he worked for people we know well, and every update I'd get from them centered around how positive, reliable, and personable he is. Communication is becoming a lost art for younger generations, and if I were to leave this earth tomorrow, I'd want to know I raised great human beings who want to positively impact others. Your kids pay close attention to how you communicate, so show them the way through positive interactions.

I Wanted to Be the Best Client

I also wanted to focus on being the best client for everyone who provides me with services, whether it's my barber or my legal professional. I didn't just want to be the positive person they interact with—I wanted to be their top referral source. I've spent so much of my career building my business through other people's networks, and now I want to help build others' businesses through mine. When you approach service relationships with this mindset, the quality of service you receive increases tenfold.

I encourage you, next time you sit down for a haircut or any service, to ask, "How can I help you grow your business?" And then, whatever their answer is, follow through. If they want referrals, I'm their guy. If they want a Google review or for me to vote for them in an award, I'll do it. I want them to see my name on their calendar and be excited to see me.

Unfortunately, we often go into service interactions expecting the worst. We assume the service provider is guilty until proven innocent. When you sit down at a restaurant and get great service, it's almost shocking because we're used to assuming they'll be annoyed or unhelpful. I used to feel the same way, but I shifted my mentality to assume everyone is innocent until proven guilty. Now, I assume I'll get great service, that they want me to be friendly, and that they'll be friendly in return.

Once again, I've noticed that this exchange of energy can lift someone's spirits, and it often encourages them to give more to others. It's almost addictive—to be abnormal, to focus on positively influencing the energy of others.

RAK: Random Act of Kindness

The final form of giving back is performing random acts of kindness. Amanda and I wanted to impact complete strangers in a different way. We started discussing various charities and nonprofits we could donate to, and we both had the same thoughts. We concluded that while donating $50,000 to a specific charity would feel great, it wouldn't provide the kind of personal impact we were looking for. That's not to say we don't still support our church or organizations we believe in, but we wanted to go in a different direction for new ideas.

We put it down on paper and realized that instead of giving $36,500 to an organization, we could give away $100 every single day to a random stranger, which would have the same economic value. I understand that giving money away to a stranger isn't a charitable deduction but that didn't matter to us. That small gesture could change the lives of 365 people, who might, in turn, impact at least one or two others. This way, we could positively influence a thousand people over time. We didn't want to start too extreme and make it unsustainable, so we applied the same structure to this idea that we've used for other ventures: first, we clarified the vision; second, we identified the best strategy; and third, we built in accountability.

We decided to start small to see how it would go. Every month, we each began giving away $100 as a starting point, and now we do it every two weeks. What we do is take $100 cash and include a letter that says:

*This money is for you. You can do whatever you want with it. We ask for nothing in return, except that you pay it forward to three people. First, send a text message to someone who has made an impact on you in the past to thank them and explain the impact they made. Second, message someone who is **currently** making* *an impact on your life, someone who may not even realize how important they've become to you—whether it's a co-worker, friend, family member, or child, it doesn't matter. Finally, reach out to someone who might need to hear from you today."*

I know it's a risky move, but I also provide my cell phone number in the letter and tell them that if they feel comfortable sharing how the experience made them feel, I'd love to hear it. If they don't want to share, I completely understand. The only rule for choosing who to give the money to is that we can't already know the person—it has to be a complete stranger, based on our gut instinct.

Some of the messages I've received in return have been incredible. For privacy reasons, I've blocked out the numbers, but here's the message I received from the first person I gave the money to:

Hello! This is Dawn from Bowlero! I just wanted to thank you so much for the financial blessing you gave me a few weeks ago! Sorry it's taken me a minute to text you! I just wanted to let you know that I was short on money to plate my vehicle for the last couple of months. Your gift helped me make up the shortfall and still have enough left over to take my daughter/granddaughter out to lunch!

But the money wasn't even the best part. It was the reflection it inspired about the people in my life. I'm so grateful that it gave me pause to honor those who have made, and are currently making, an impact in my life. It also opened my eyes to those around me who might need a little pick-me-up or an encouraging message. Those messages lifted my heart and spirits more than you'll ever know or than I can put into words.

Thank you for giving me this opportunity to reflect on life at a time when my world was a little dark (in April, it will be two years since I lost my mom). May God bless you and your family, and thank you for adding light back into my life!

$100 isn't an insane amount of money, but I believe it can change how someone views life. The mission of this final chapter is to inspire you by showing that your energy matters. How you show up every day can influence many people. I want to win the battle of which energy is being mirrored. If I can do that and bring energy and smiles to those around me, it makes me feel infinitely wealthy.

In this book, I've tried to identify ways for you to redesign your future. The main mission is to provide tools and techniques to help anyone become successful in their career while also being "rich" at home. I want to reverse the course of being successful in what we do but broke at home. I was on that path, and I couldn't be more thankful to everyone—whether I've mentioned them in this book or not—for saving my life.

To Amanda and my kids, I fight every day to show you how much I love you and how much we can impact the world, one person at a time.

Action Items

1. Reach out to someone from the past that had a massive impact on you, thank them and tell them what impact they made. Who was it and how did they respond?

   _____

   _____

   _____

   _____

   _____

2. Reach out to someone who is impacting you now. Who was it, and how did they respond?

   _____

   _____

   _____

   _____

   _____

3. Reach out to someone who could really use hearing from you now. Who was it, and how did they respond?

_____

_____

_____

_____

_____

_____

CONCLUSION

The main message of this book is to help people start winning at home. The way to win at home is through intentionality—being focused and present with those around you. Your focus and intention are signs of appreciation or gratitude for the people in your life. My final thoughts for the readers are simple: this works. I promise you, if you apply these steps, techniques, or mindsets consistently over time, you will see tremendous results.

Not only will you see results, but you'll also learn a lot about yourself and how to give back—how to make an impact on those around you. I almost feel like we all start in a hole, and once we dig our way out, we can turn around, extend a hand, and start pulling others out with us. We live in a very scary world right now, and I hope that with focus, processes, and intentionality, we can begin to change the world around us and how people view things.

I want to take a moment to thank anyone who invested time in reading this book. For those who already know me, your belief in me means a lot. The biggest sign of gratitude you can give me isn't a thank-you note—it's the implementation of any of these ideas or mindsets. What I truly hope is that you don't just read this and then put the book on a shelf or start a document without completing it.

It's natural to feel motivated for a short period of time after reading something, much like listening to a motivational speaker who inspires you to change your life. But if you don't act on those feelings, they'll be forgotten quickly. We forget within 24 hours over 50% of the content we hear. So, I hope this is a book you will continue to pick up and reference, finding sustainability in the changes you want to make.

For the reader, what's possible now is the realization that this is like a muscle—it takes time to build, and it needs to be worked on consistently because change is hard. It's so much easier to form a new habit than it is to break an old one. Breaking old habits is difficult.

It's easy to find yourself scrolling through social media at 10 o'clock in the morning if that's what you're used to. It's normal to go home and give your family the bottom 10% of your energy. So, it will take time—but don't give up.

Hang in there—it will work.

THANK YOU FOR READING MY BOOK!

DOWNLOAD YOUR FREE GIFTS

Just to say thanks for buying and reading my book, I've put together a welcome video along with some helpful documents to support you on your journey with the book!

Scan the QR Code:

I appreciate your interest in my book, and value your feedback as it helps me improve future versions of this book. I would appreciate it if you could leave your invaluable review on Amazon.com with your feedback. Thank you!

www.ingramcontent.com/pod-product-compliance
Lightning Source LLC
LaVergne TN
LVHW050240211224
799495LV00027B/566/J